Simon Bull
Coloring Book
Volume I, Flowers

A book of sketches for personal coloration based on the iconic floral paintings of Simon Bull.

With anecdotes and thoughts in the artist's own words.

Don't be shy, share your results with the Simon Bull Coloring Book Community!

Facebook: www.facebook.com/simonbullart
Instagram: #simonbullcoloringbook
Twitter: @Simon_Bull_Art

For more information on Simon Bull visit:
www.bullart.com

In this book, I have compiled fifty designs based on some of my most popular floral images from over the last twenty years. It has really been fun for me to revisit works from back in the day and to see how my thoughts and observations have evolved over the years.

I hope you have as much fun creating your own colored versions from these outlines as I did when I first sat in my garden, sketchbook in hand, and opened my heart to what nature had to tell me all those years ago.

Enjoy.
Simon Bull

The Journey Never Ends

This image won an award, the 2003 NALED
(National Association of Limited Edition
Dealers) Print of the Year Award to be precise.
It also featured on the cover of art magazines
and became one of my top selling pieces. That
is all cool, but for me this piece and it's title
has always held a special meaning.

While painting it I found myself being drawn,
not just into the flower but into some strange
new world beyond it's spreading wings. It
is this world, beyond the visual surface that
I now invite you, through the pages of this
book, to explore. Let your imagination take
off from here!

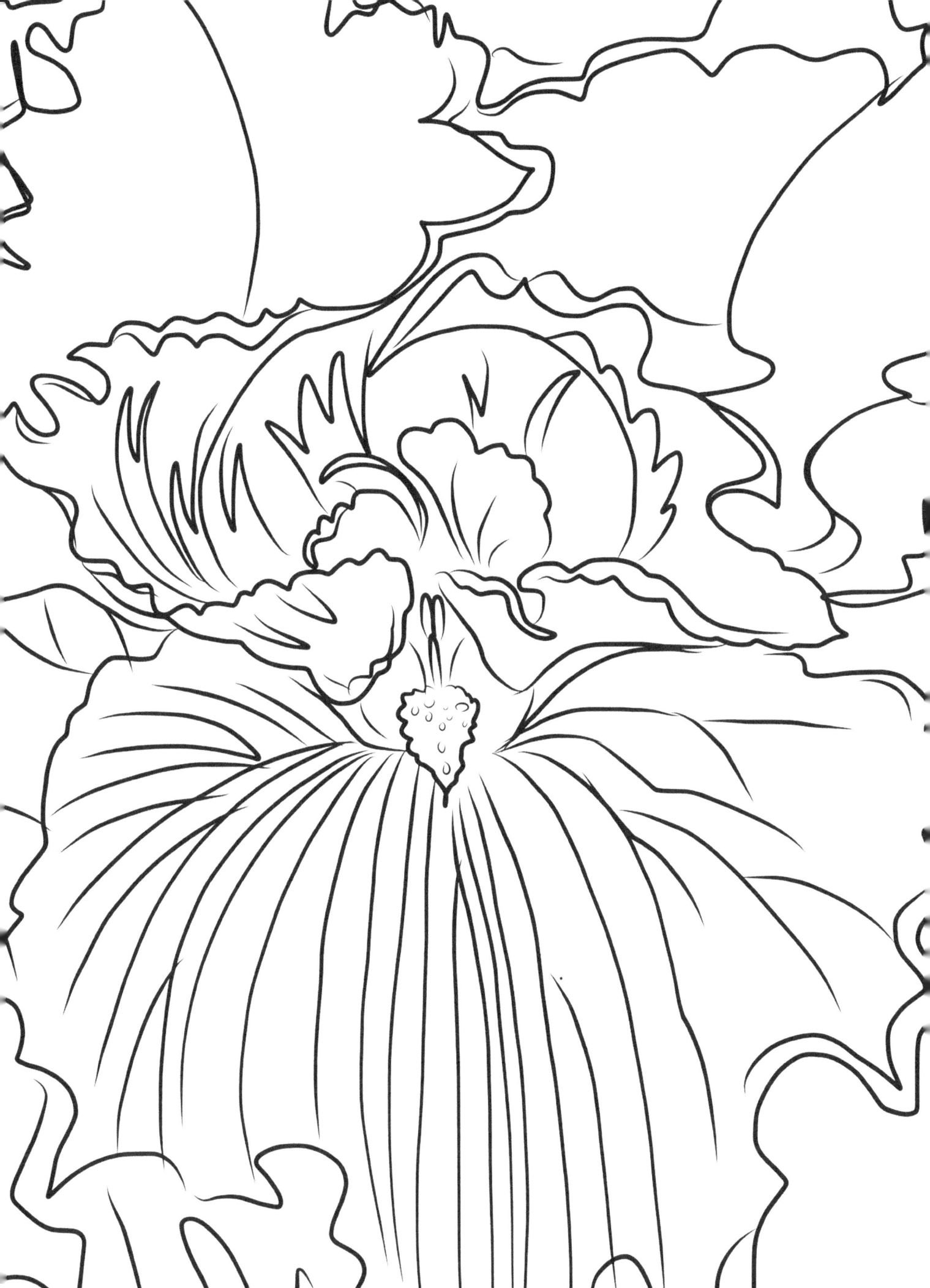

Sealed with a Kiss

From the trembling thrill of a 'first kiss' to the
passionate entwining of lover's lips, kisses have
been bringing us together and helping us say
goodbye since the beginning of time. A kiss
says something, it confirms something and
it can feel like, wow, really something! So go
ahead, confirm your love and seal your love -
with a kiss.

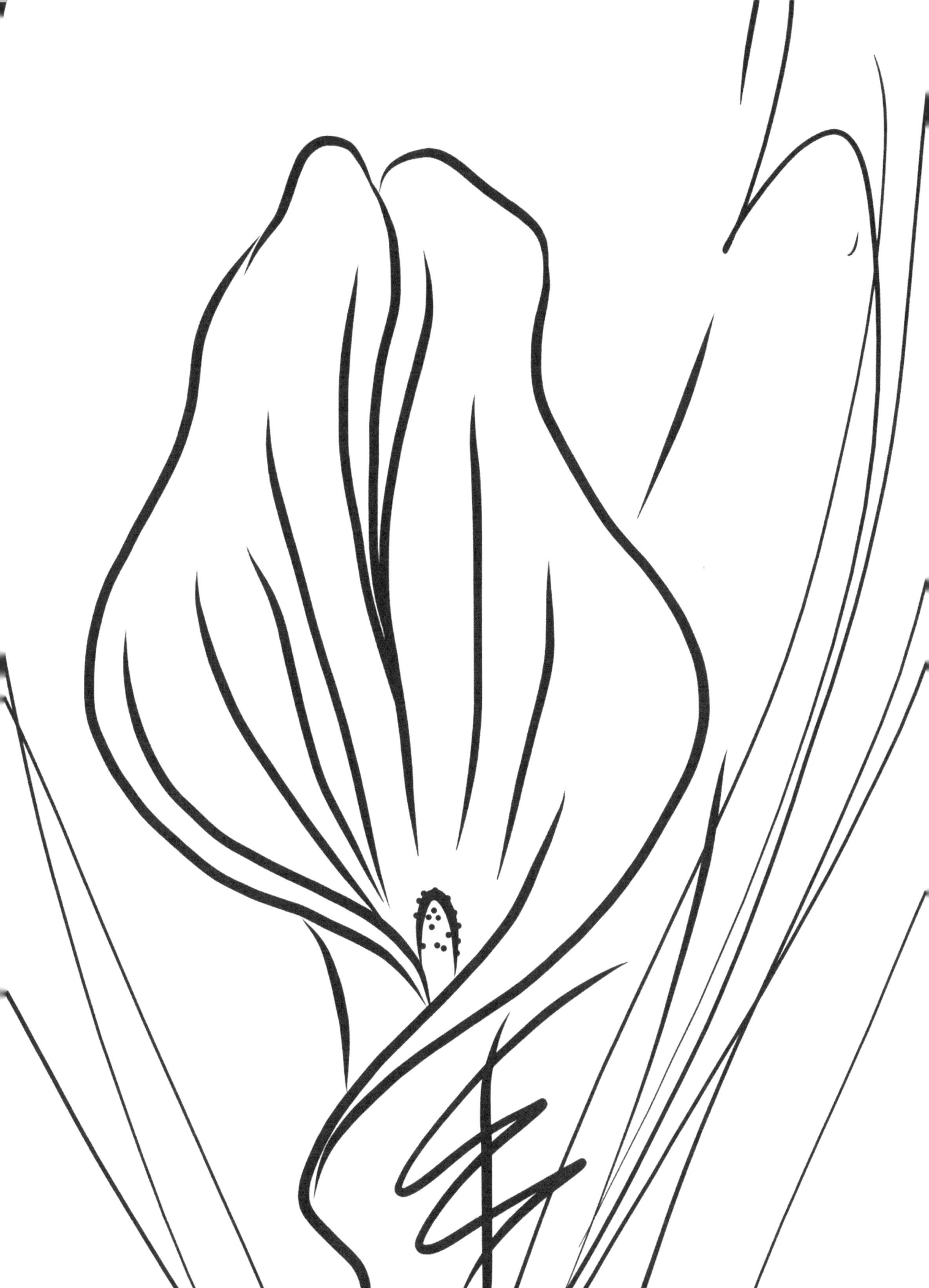

All the Way to Paradise

This is a family portrait. It actually started
life as a commission. The family that asked
for it had just been to Hawaii on vacation and
wanted a painting of orchids to remind them
of their trip and to symbolize them as a family
in some way.

The painting speaks about the joy of life in
all it's stages, whilst acknowledging that even
death itself is only another step, a step into
paradise where all the burdens and sorrows of
life will be finally washed away in the eternity
of God's love. The best is yet to come.

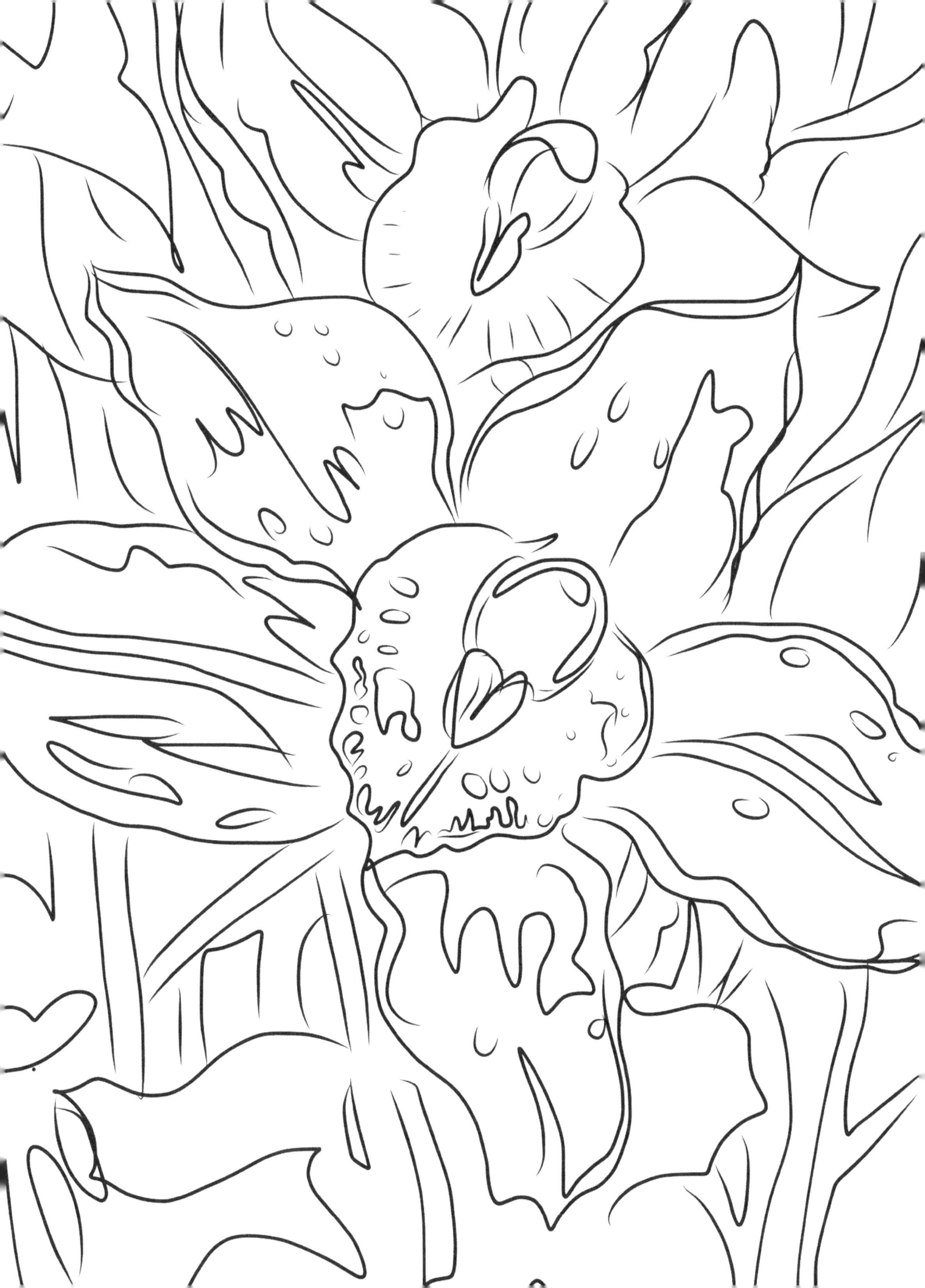

More than a Song

When I was child I attended Ripon Cathedral
Choir school in England. I loved and still do
love singing, Singing does for the ear what art
does for the eyes, but ultimately it is what it
conveys to our heart that matters most.

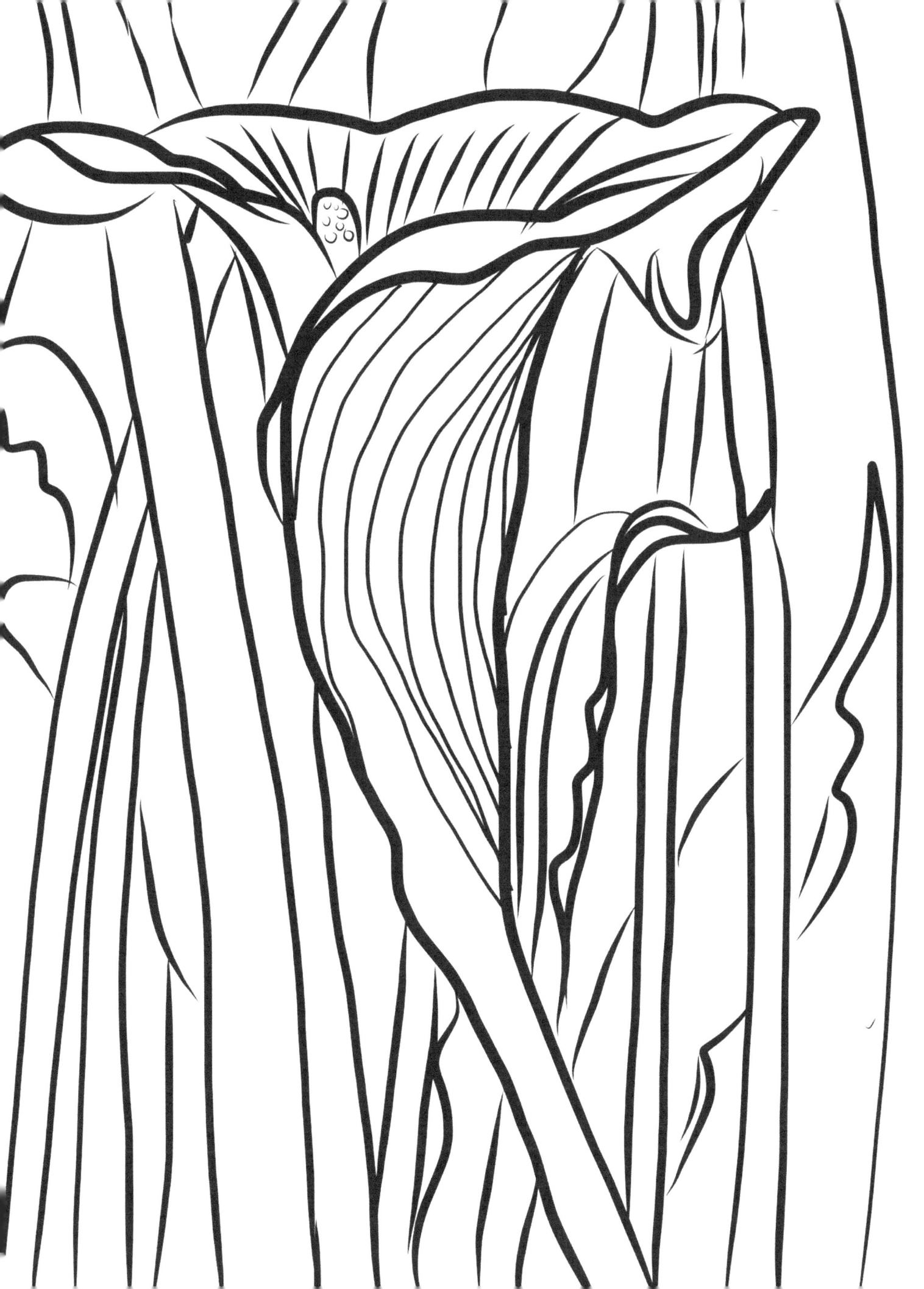

Dreams

There are dreams that we follow, even though
we cannot see where they may lead. Follow-
ing a star can sometimes be lonely, but if we
can find another soul to join us on our quest,
the way becomes brighter and success more
certain.

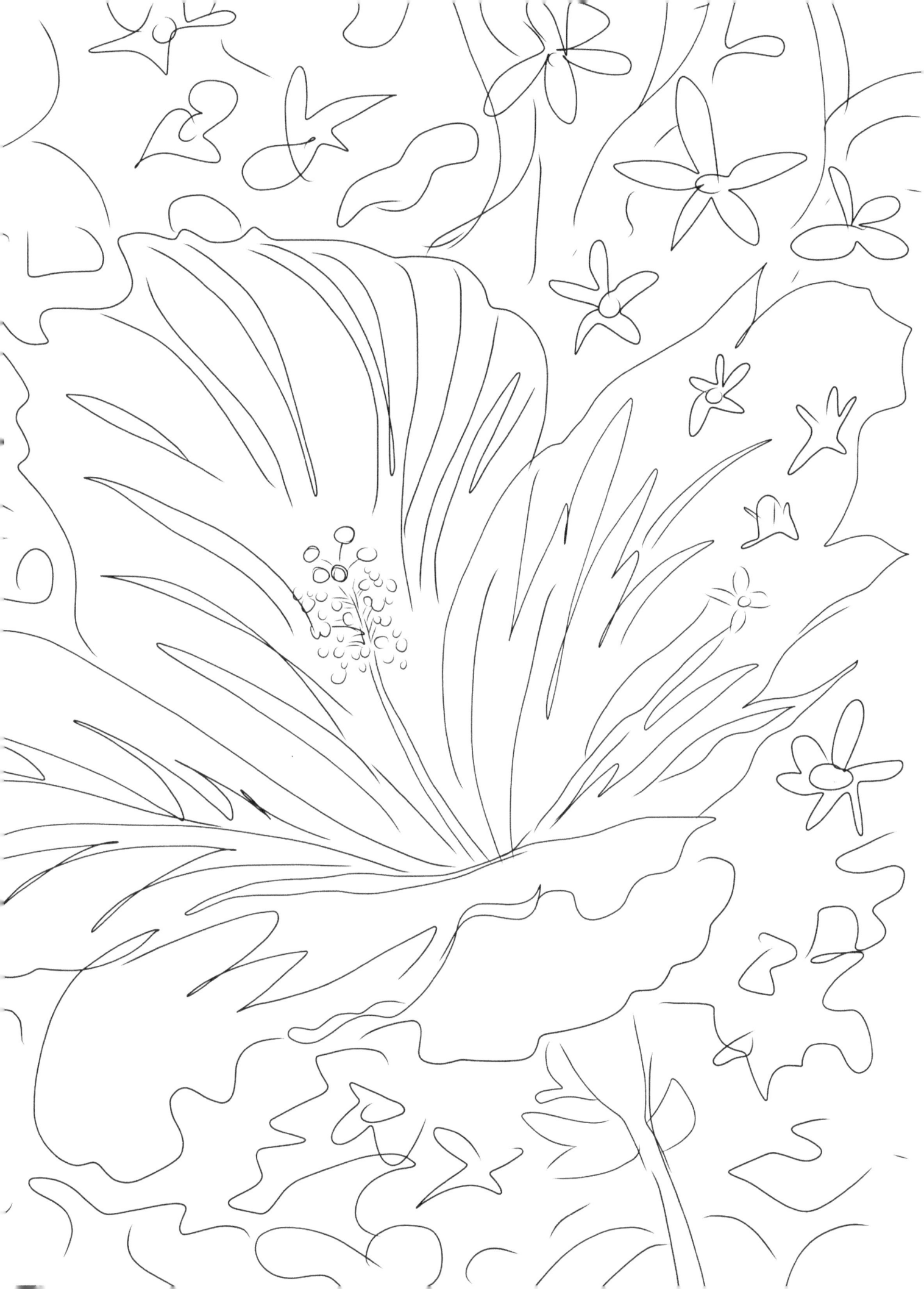

Lighter Than Air

Drawn by intoxicating fragrance, a butterfly shimmers in the morning sunlight as it dances, lighter than air, among pollen-dusted flowers. Absorbed by its own activity and unaware that the flowers depend on this fleeting visitor for their own passive but captivating life-cycle.

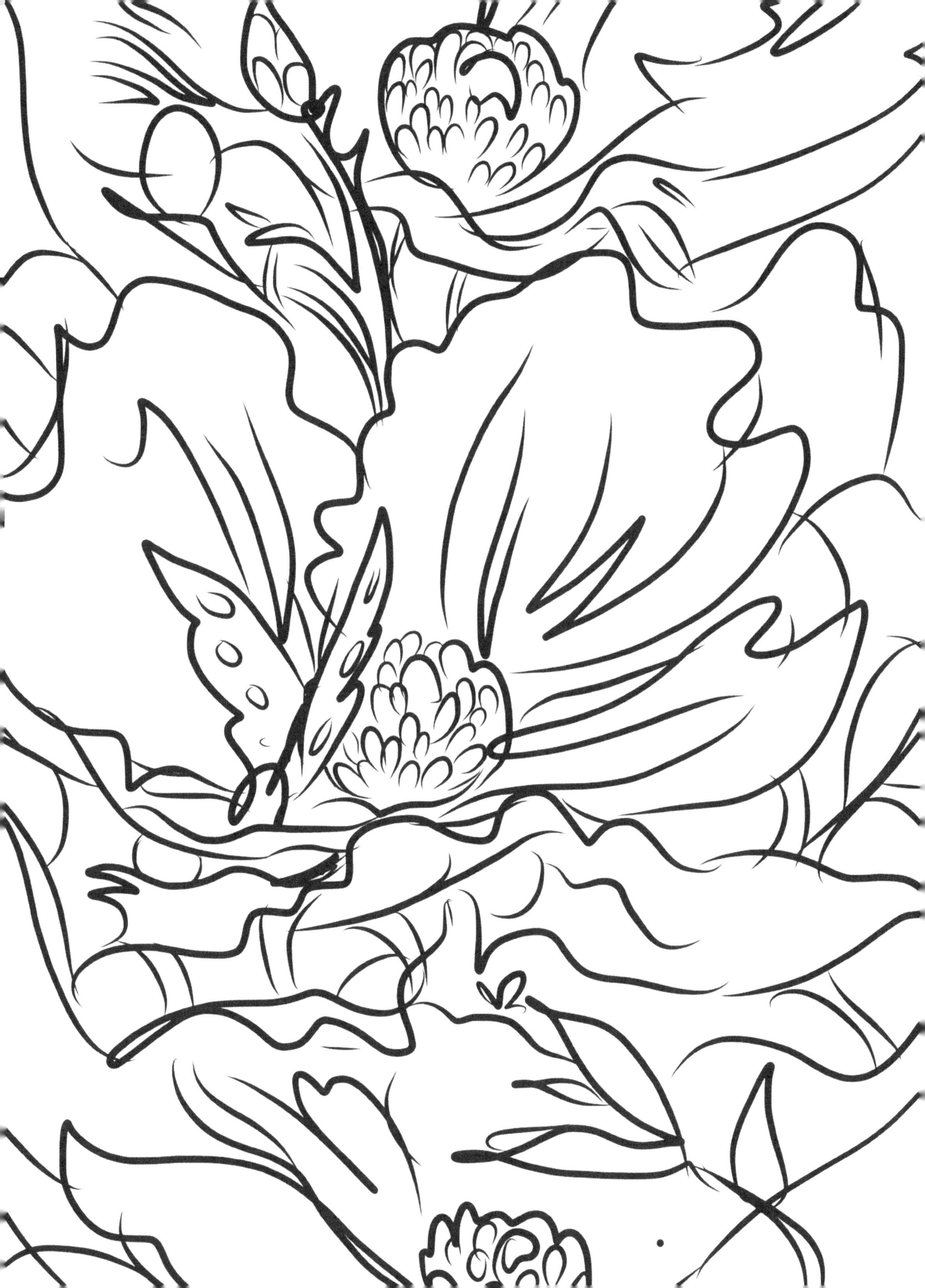

Blazing Red

Truth really is better than fiction in many
ways, which is why I still base nearly all my
flower paintings on something seen. I start
with an initial thought and take it for a walk as
I paint.

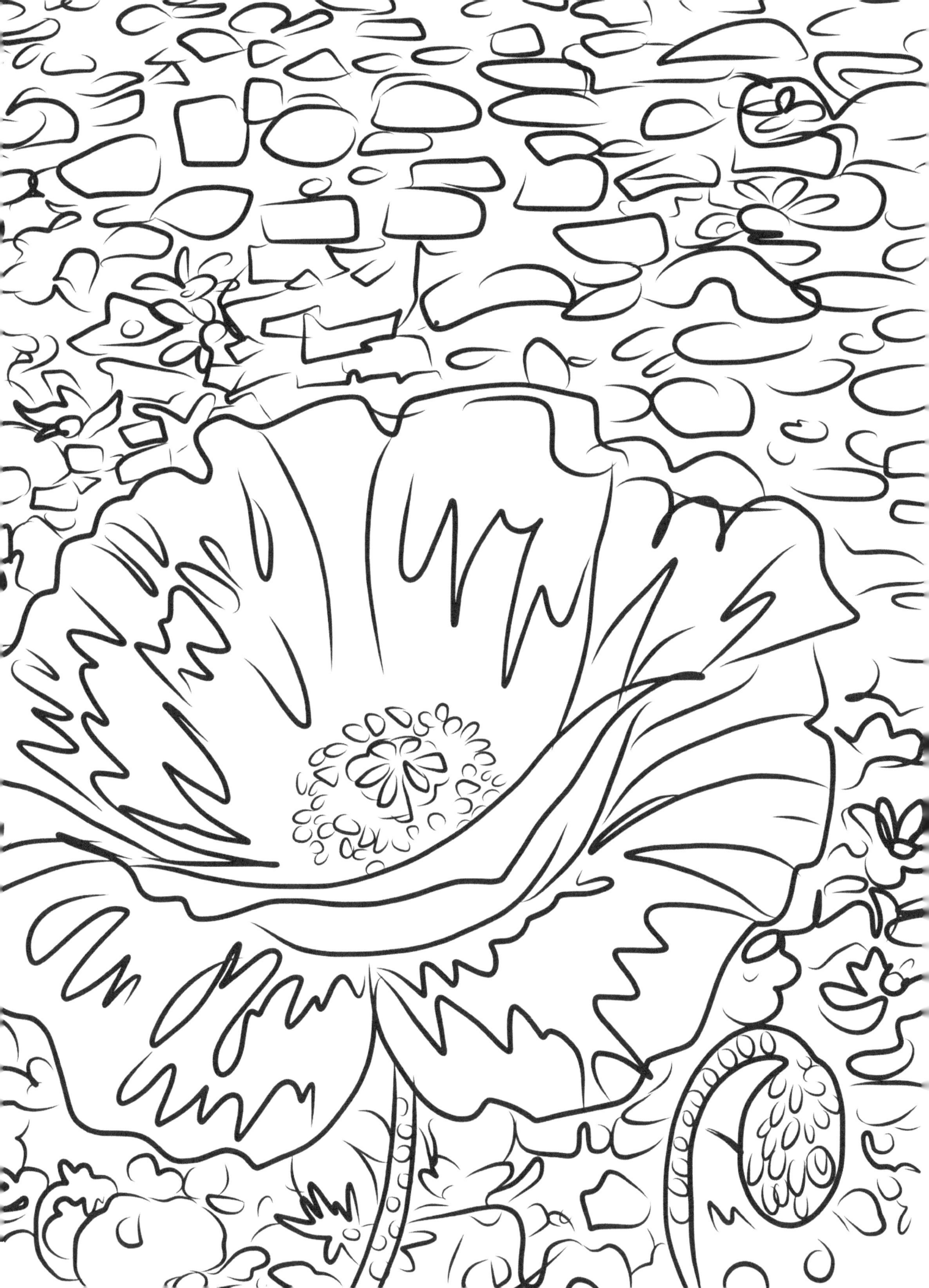

Journey

This is a sketch from a small portion of the
largest painting I have completed to date. It
was seventeen feet long and four foot six inch-
es high. I have turned it on its side to fit this
book and think it works well this way around.
See if you can make it look even better.

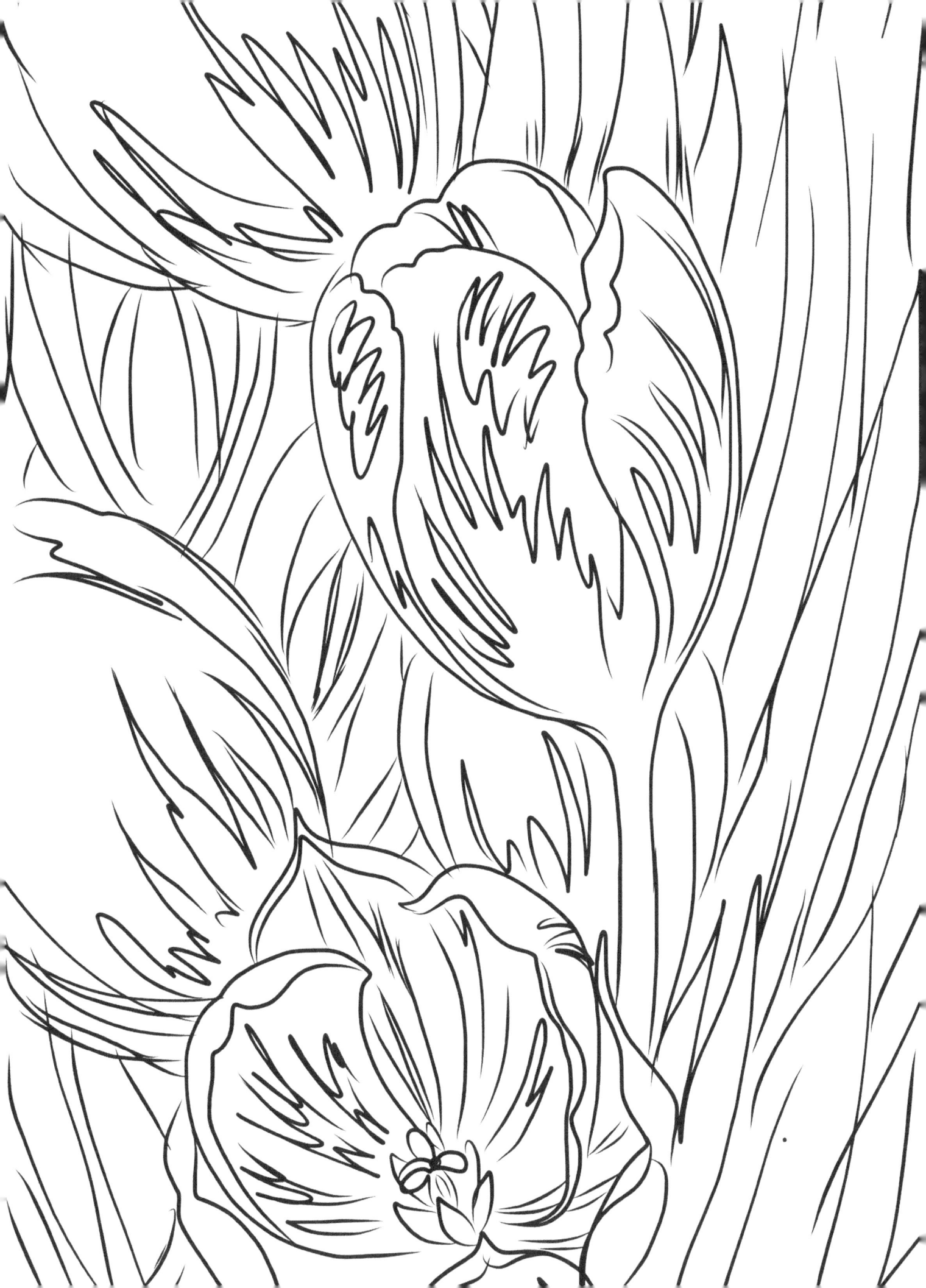

In Your Light

The Matilija poppy has long been one of my
favorite flowers. I first came across it many
years ago in the gardens of Ripley Castle in
England where I was painting flowers for an
exhibition in London. Since it is not native to
England the flower struck me as exotic, but
now that I live on the Monterey Peninsula
I am surrounded by them all the time. Fa-
miliarity however, has increased rather than
diminished my appreciation for these delicate
and expressive flowers that waft in the breeze
like angels throughout the warm days of early
summer

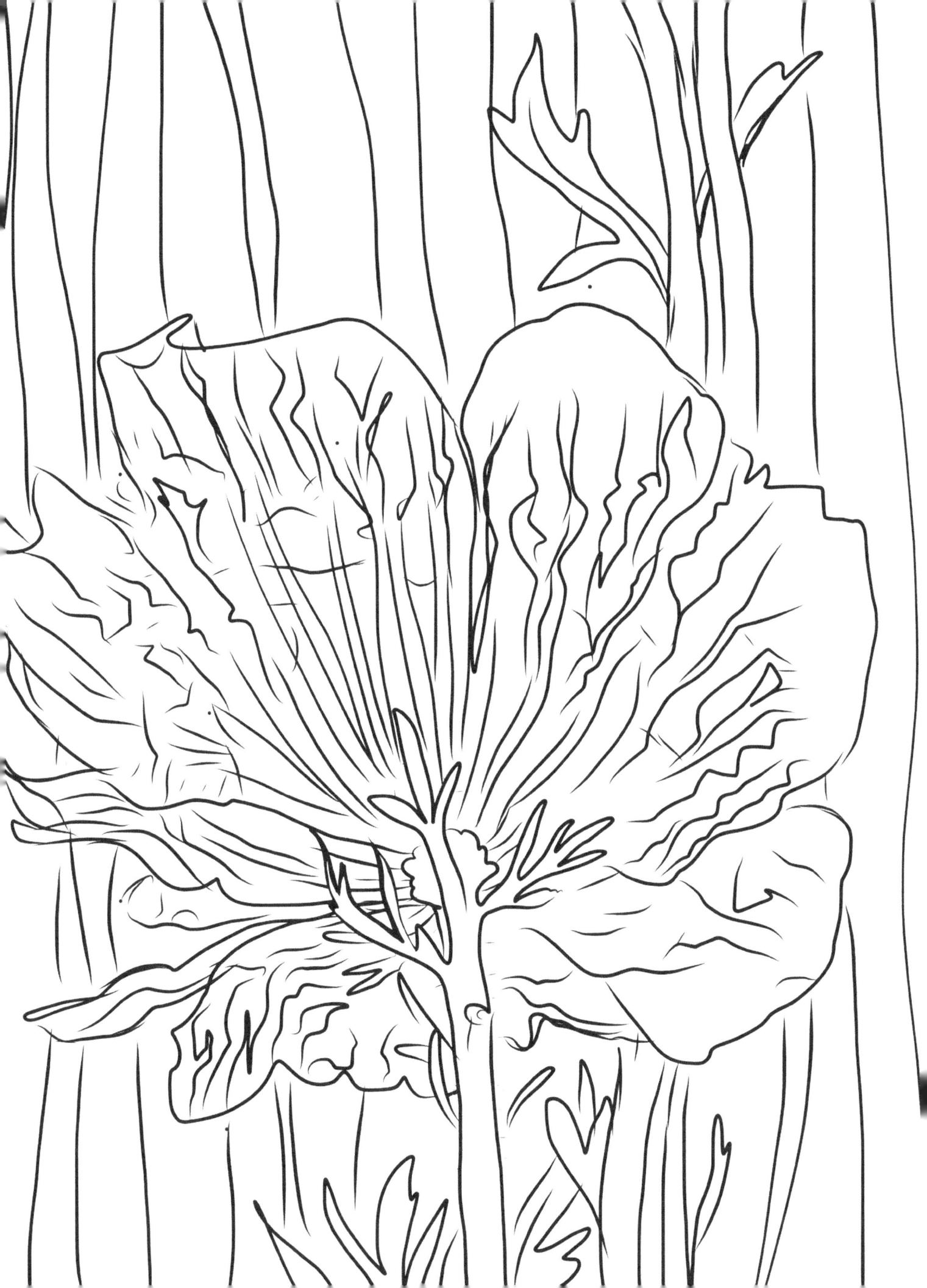

Place in the Sun

All plants grow according to a mathematical
formula known as the Fibonacci Series, in bot-
any the more specific form of the sequence is
known as Phyllotactic spiral. That all sounds a
littl complicated but what it amounts to is that
once a leaf of petal emerges from the stem, it
looks for the place with the most exposure to
sunlight and settles there. As each new leaf
grows a spiral pattern emerges, which, when
viewed from directly above looks like a spiral
star shape.

Sunlight is essential to life and throughout our
years we all lean to eventually find our own
place in the sun.

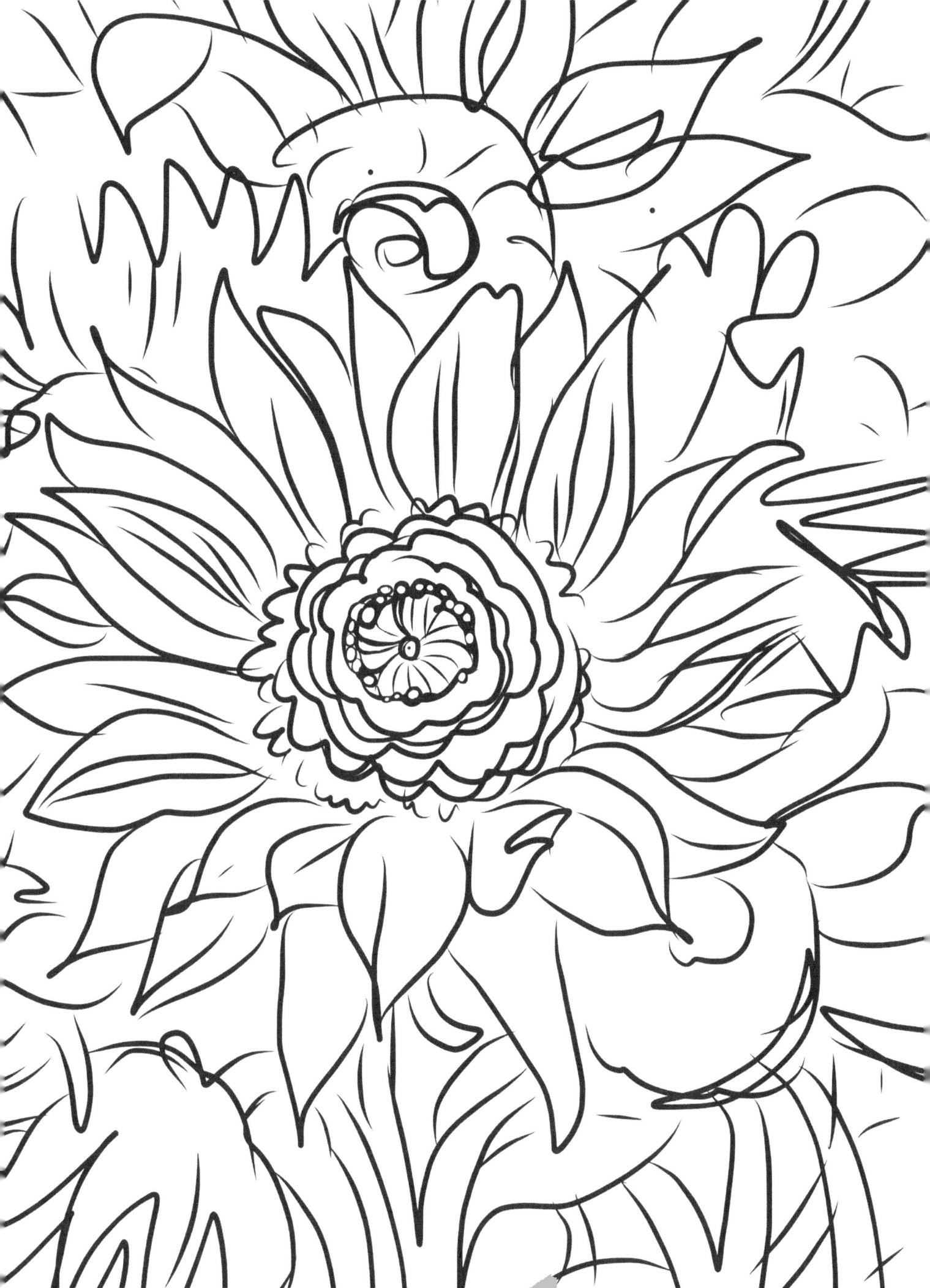

Perfume

Delicate like lace, or billows of silk lifted by
invisible breezes, richly clothed like a bride
or winged like an angel, fragrant, ephemeral,
fleeting. This is the Matilija poppy in all its
enigmatic beauty.

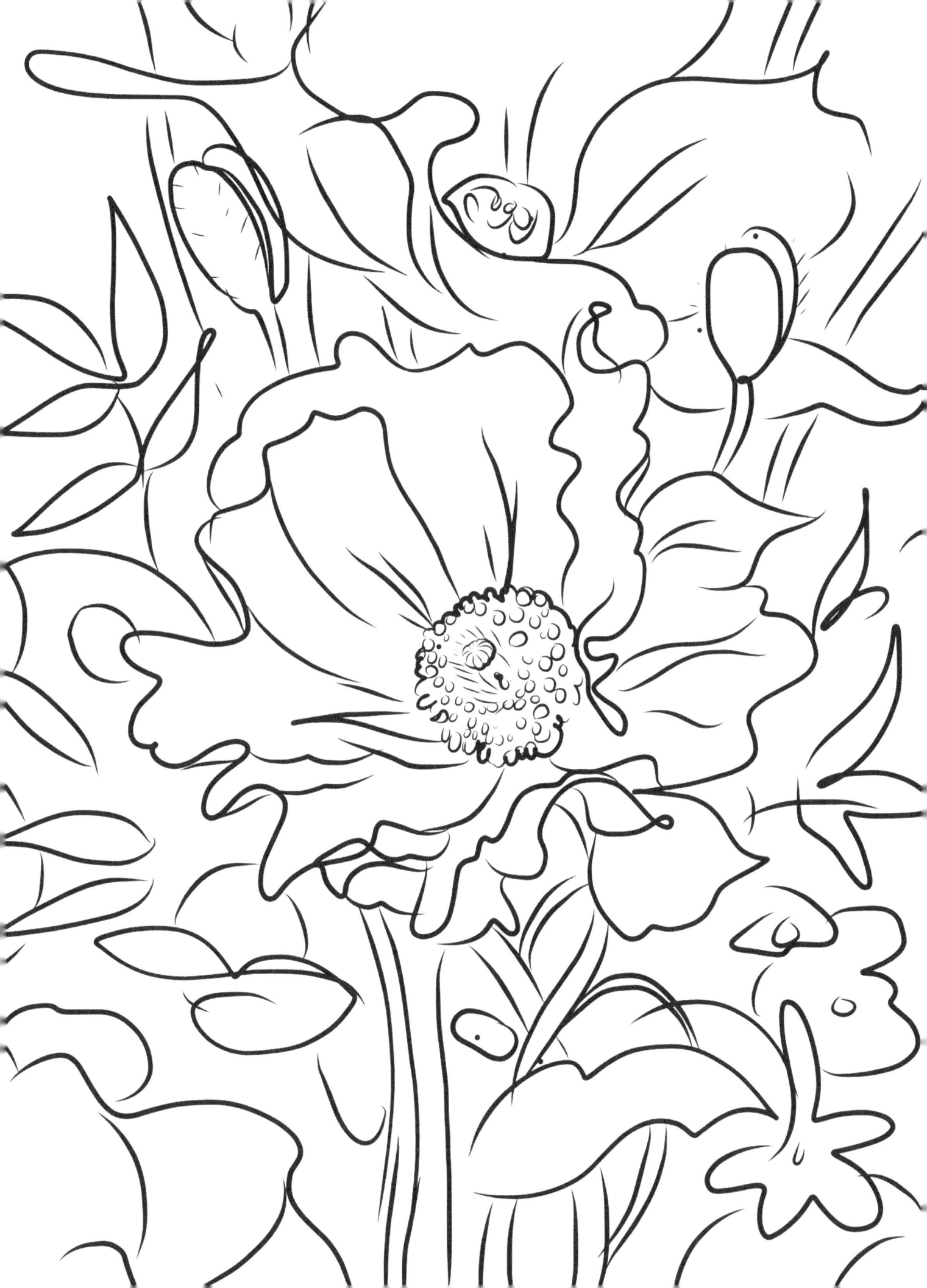

Beautiful Dreamer

Whenever I draw flowers I notice that, even
if I concentrate intently on one bloom, there
is always something else happening in the
picture around it. I love all that other noise,
after all isn't it all part of that bigger picture we
call life?

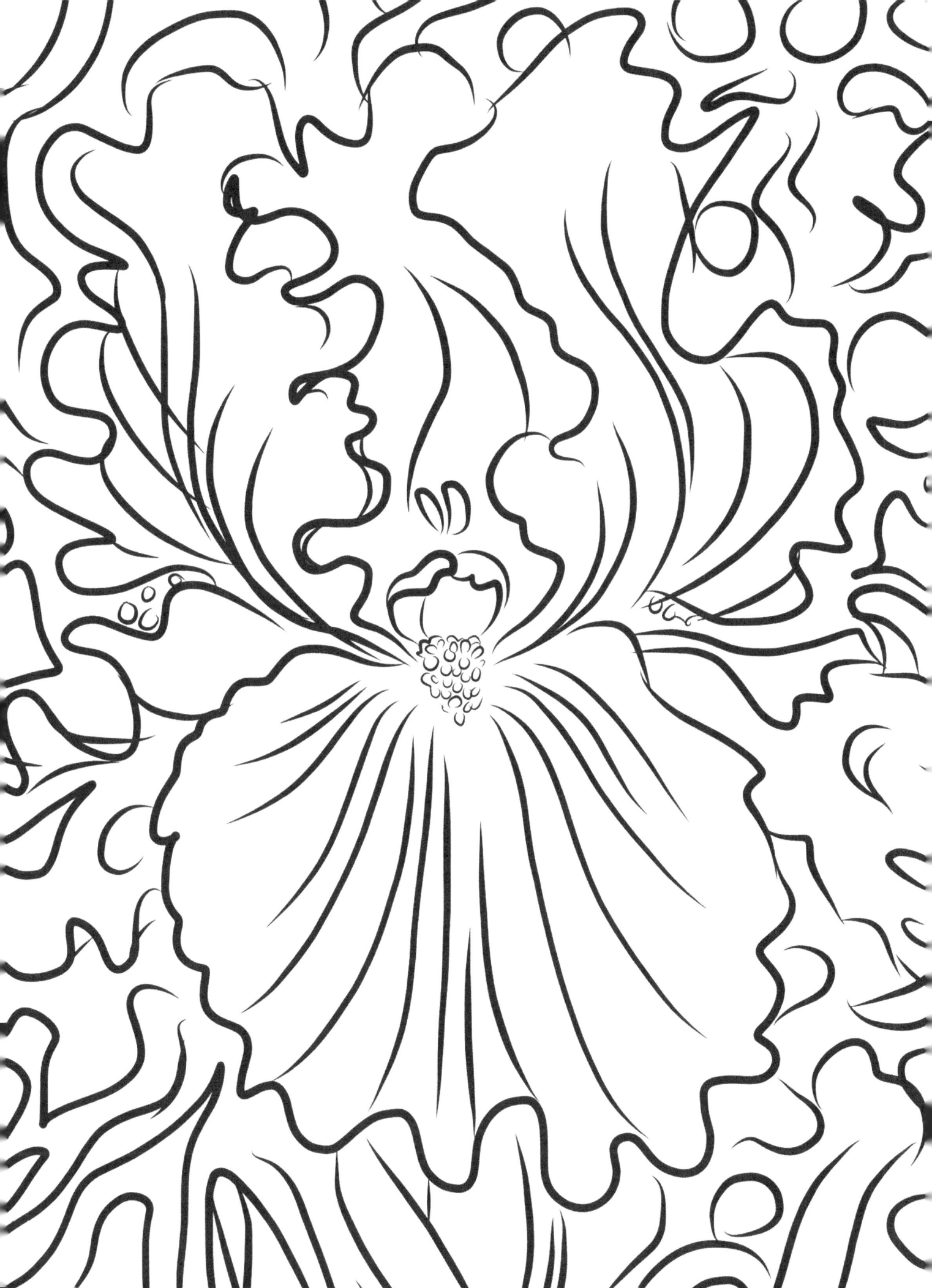

Tulips

Did you know that the tulip was once the most
expensive commodity on earth? We have the
Dutch to thank for that and maybe they were
not so wrong.

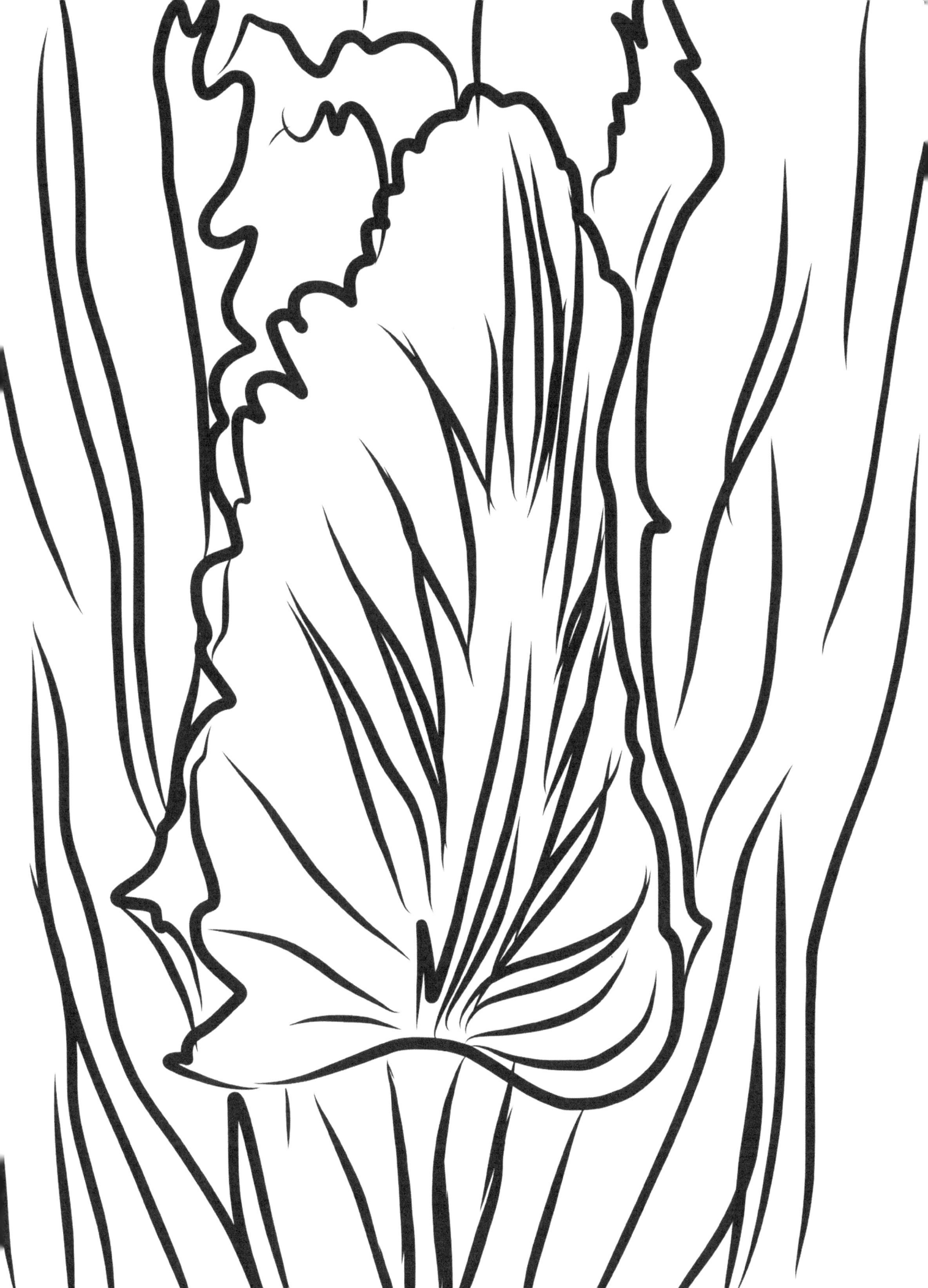

In a Heartbeat

I found this beautiful poppy while out draw-
ing in my garden. The half open, chalice like
flower, unfolding in the morning light, attract-
ed my attention and instantly led me to make
a series of studies that eventually became "in
a Heartbeat". I never cease to be amazed at the
startling diversity and variety in nature.

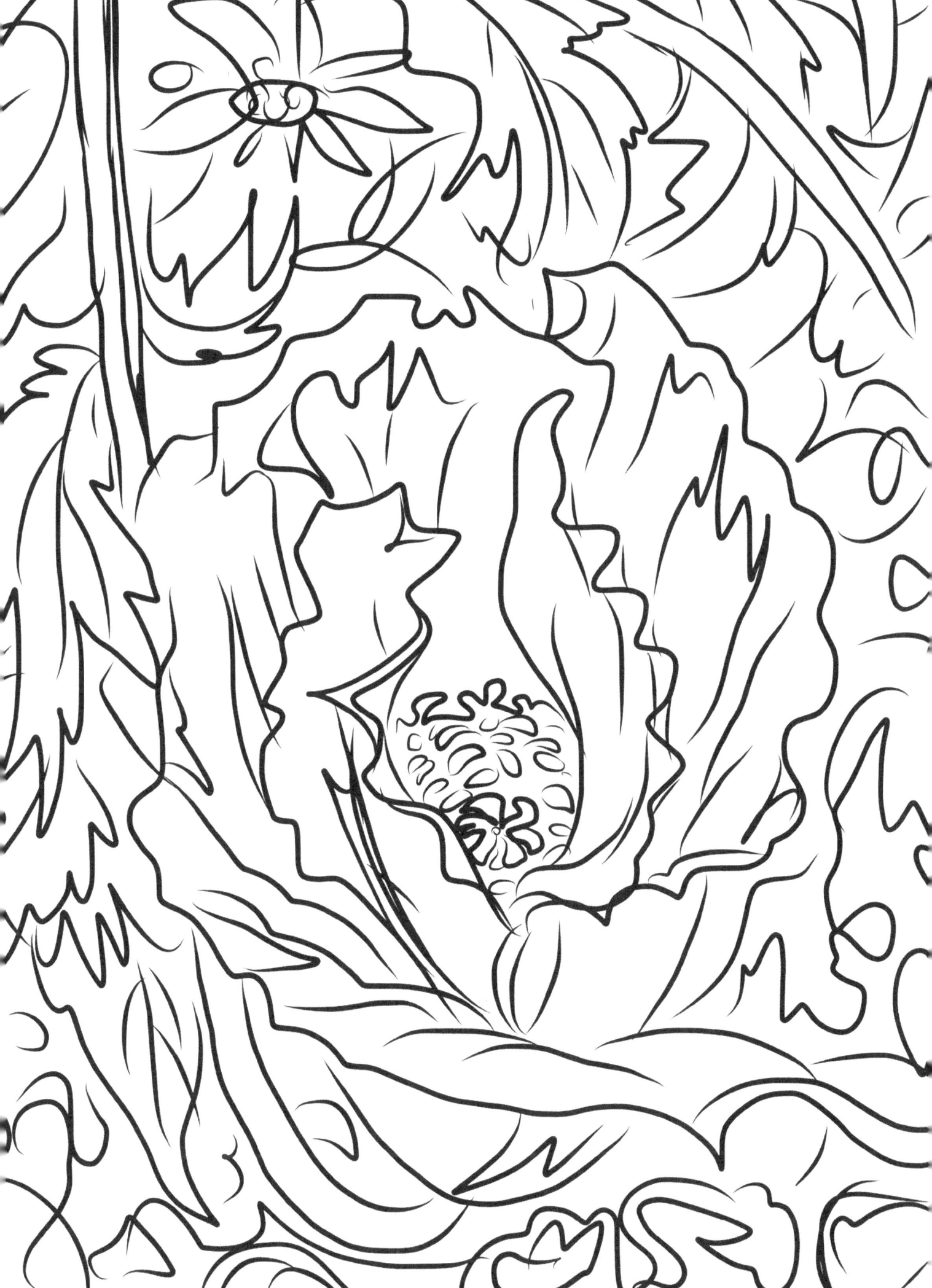

A Star is Born

Andy Warhol once said that "In the future everyone will be world-famous for fifteen minutes." It was one of those crazy saying that was so strange it became memorable. It also made those who heard it feel more significant, less lost and in a tiny way offered a ray of hope into our apparently obscure lives. Flowers do something similar, they are here today and gone tomorrow and yet their sheer beauty prompts us to think that surely, in their own small way flowers also have their fifteen minutes of fame their moment of immortality.

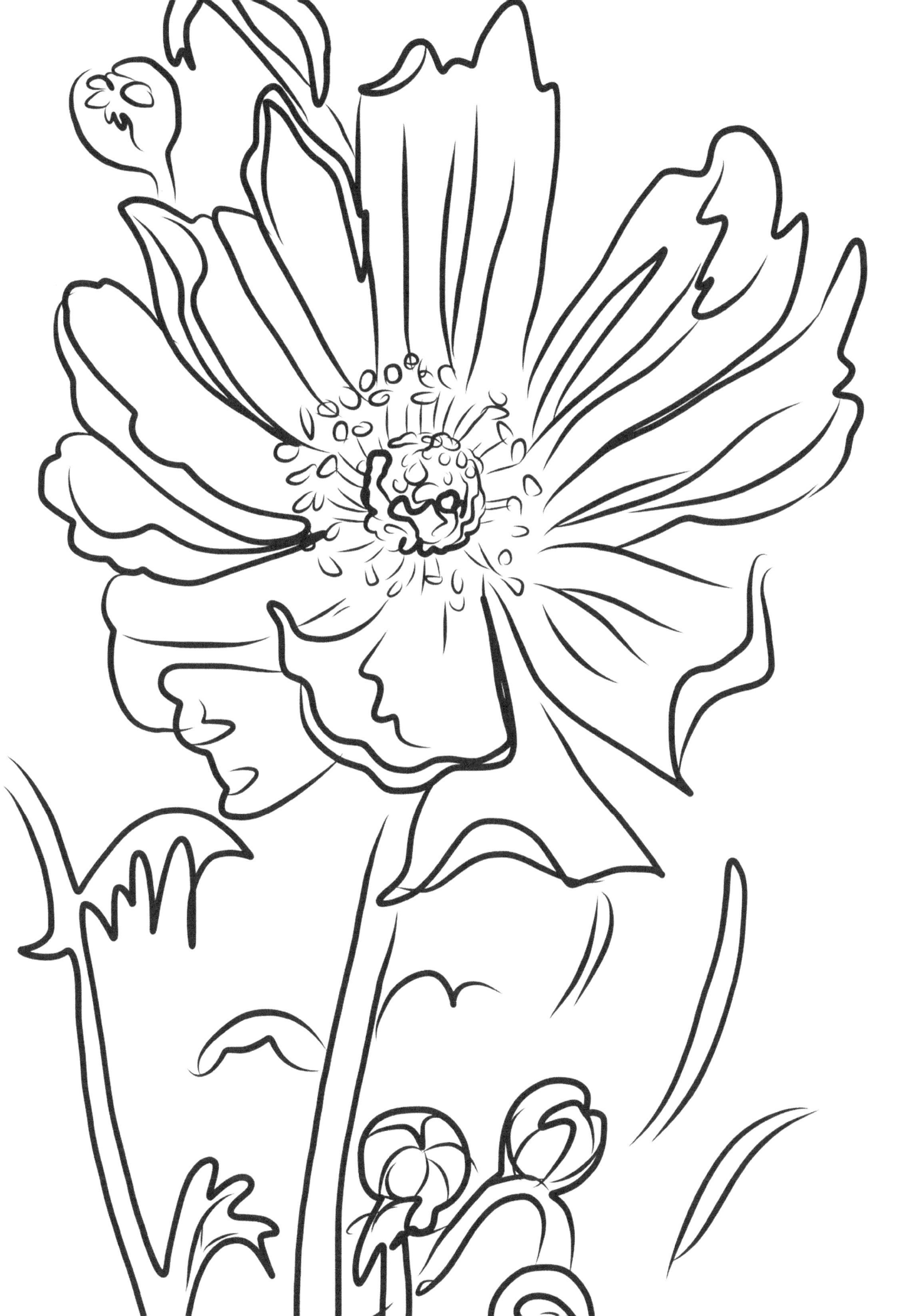

First Love

The idea of "First Love" is often associated
with our first date or kiss. It reminds us of the
time we took that first shy walk in the park or
watched a movie with someone special. In this
sense first love was full of wonder, excitement
and apprehension, it was often also shallow
and self centered. But there is a deeper kind
of first love, namely the kind that is first, not
because of its place in the chronology of our
lives but that which is first in our hearts, first
in importance, the true love of our life.

There are times when the hectic pace of life
can take our focus away from the one, or the
ones we love and cherish the most. This ren-
dition of a simple daisy extends an invitation
to us all: return to your first love, stop hiding
your feelings, now is the time.

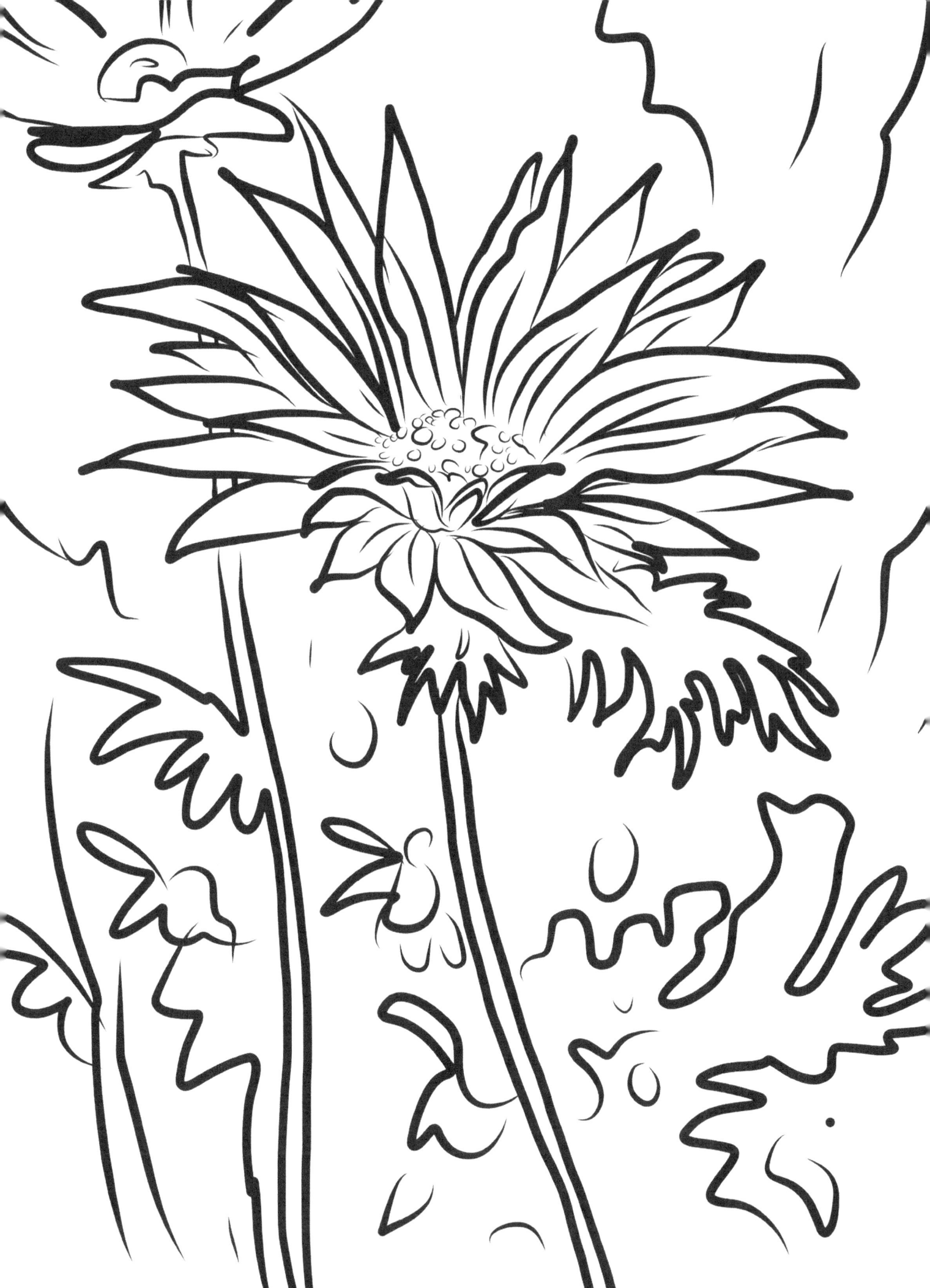

Fantasia

One of the great things about painting is that you are not limited to rendering reality like a camera; you can take your imagery from anywhere and change it any way you want. In my painting of this I took the delicate and normally white Calla lily and infused it with hot, vibrant reds. See what you can do with it!

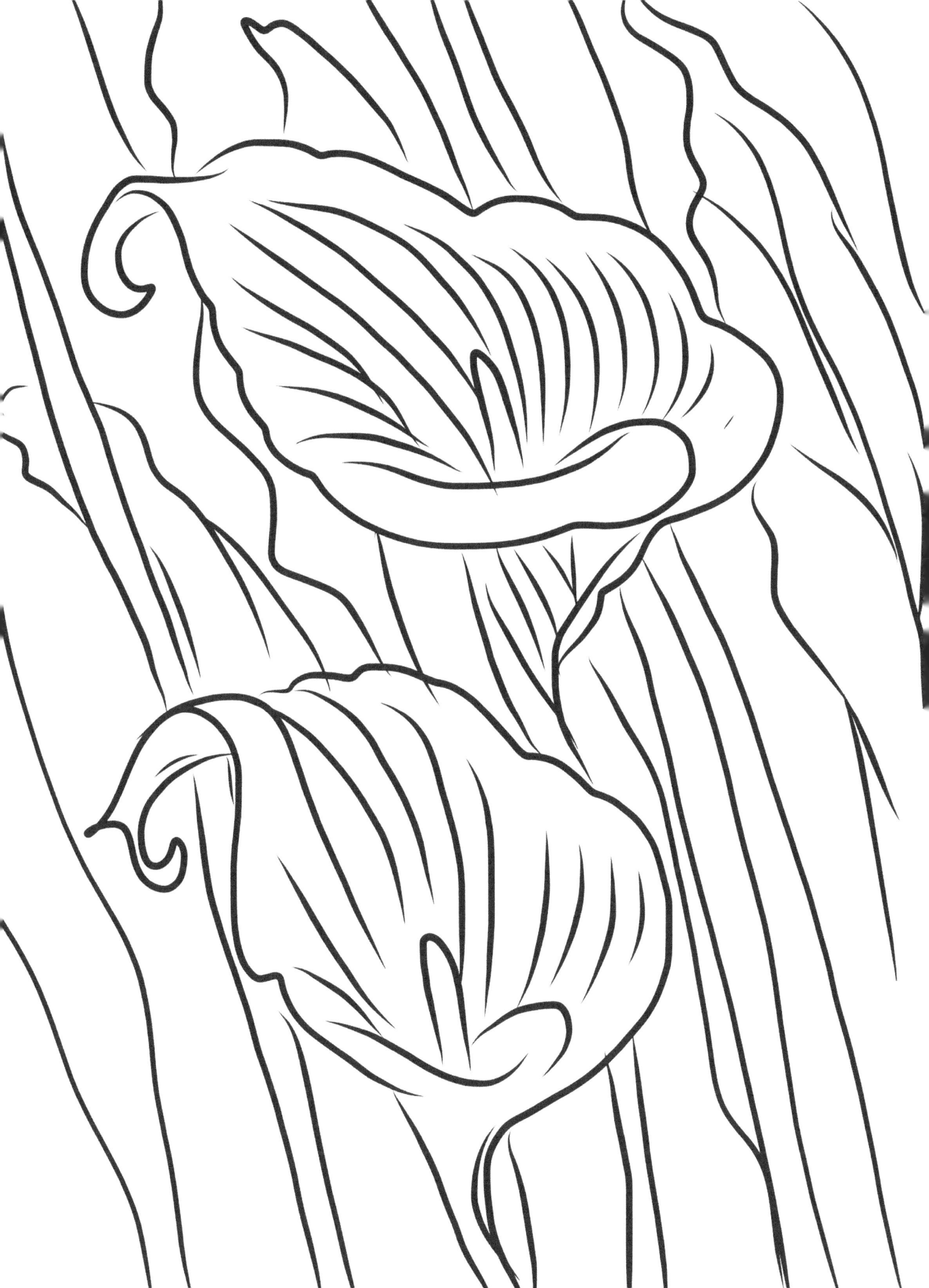

Your Beauty Lies Within You

First impressions can be very important and
in a new relationship we are always keen to
put our best side to the fore. However, as each
day goes by the 'real' person inside starts to
show and we inevitably see each others faults
and weaknesses. We know when we are truly
loved when someone accepts us as we are and
embraces us 'warts and all'.
The poppy in Your beauty Lies Within You
suggests this unveiling as its petals open to the
sun to reveal the black as well as the red, the
dark and the light which together create a fully
rounded vision of beauty, beauty that is more
than skin deep.

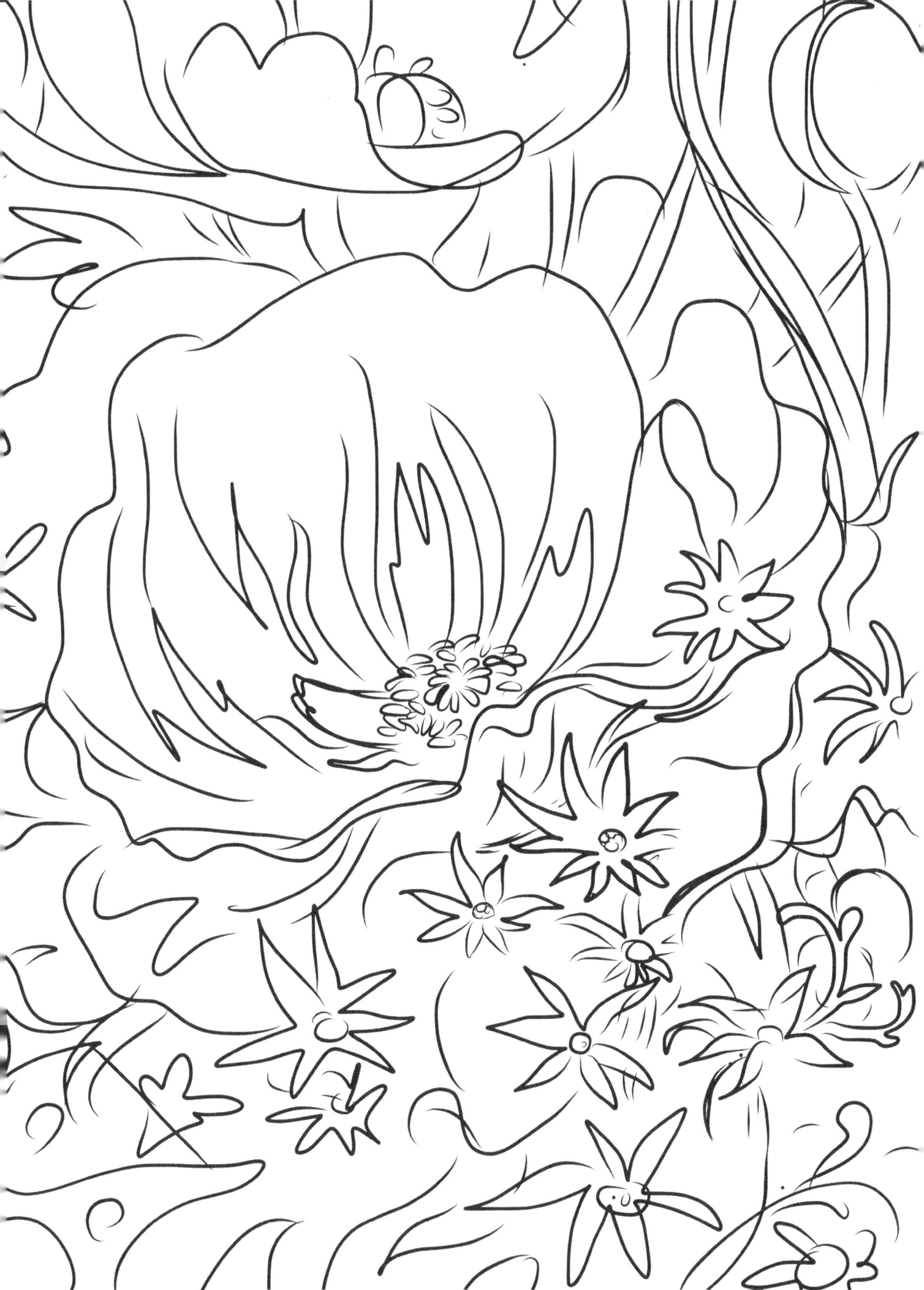

Because of You

Because of who you are, and what you mean
to me. Because of all you have done for me,
because of all the times we have shared together and the tough times we have gone through.
Because of all these things and more, I offer
this…

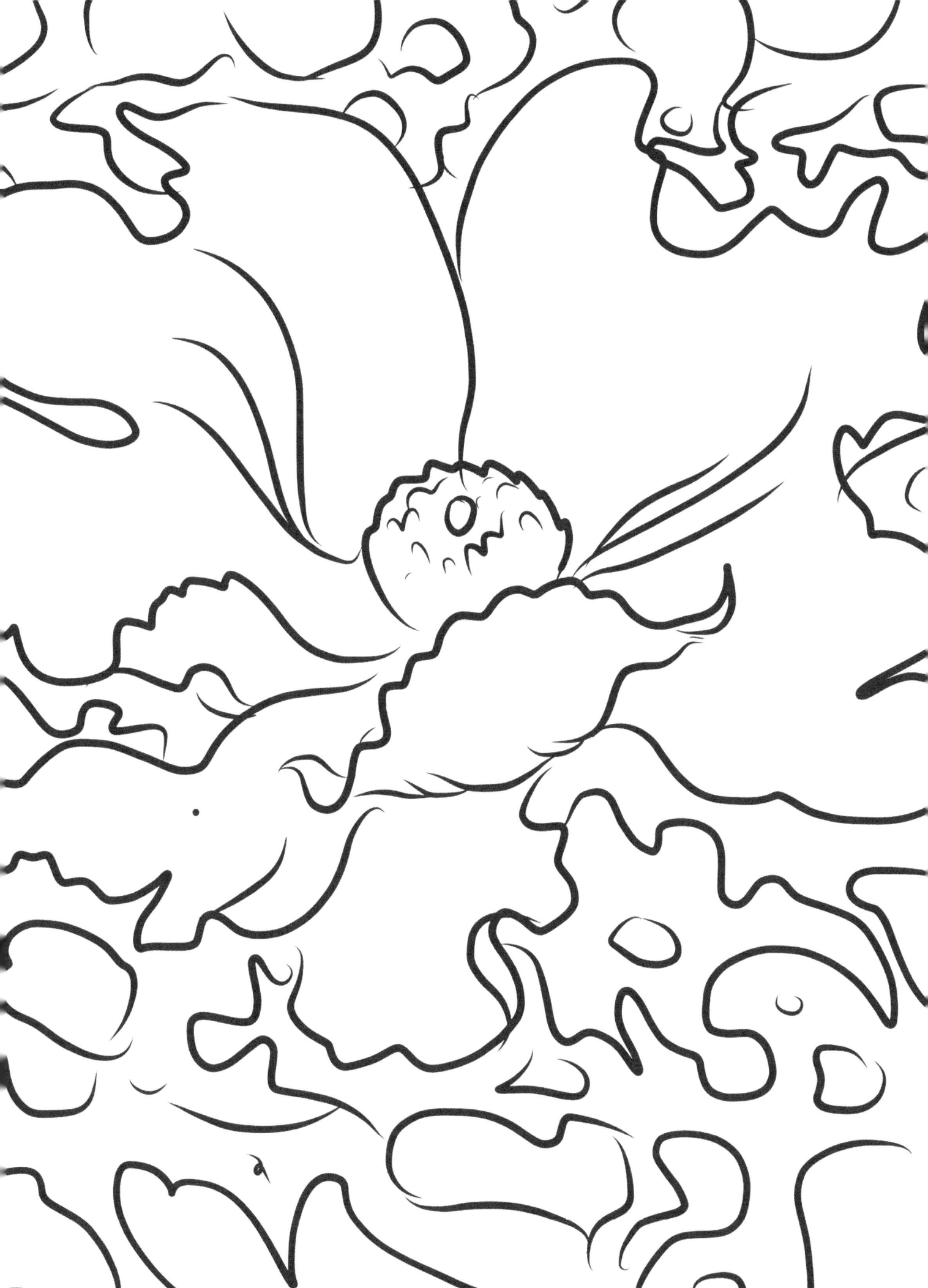

In Your Light

Have you ever seen a plant growing down-
wards towards the dark earth? No. They were
born for the light, as were we.

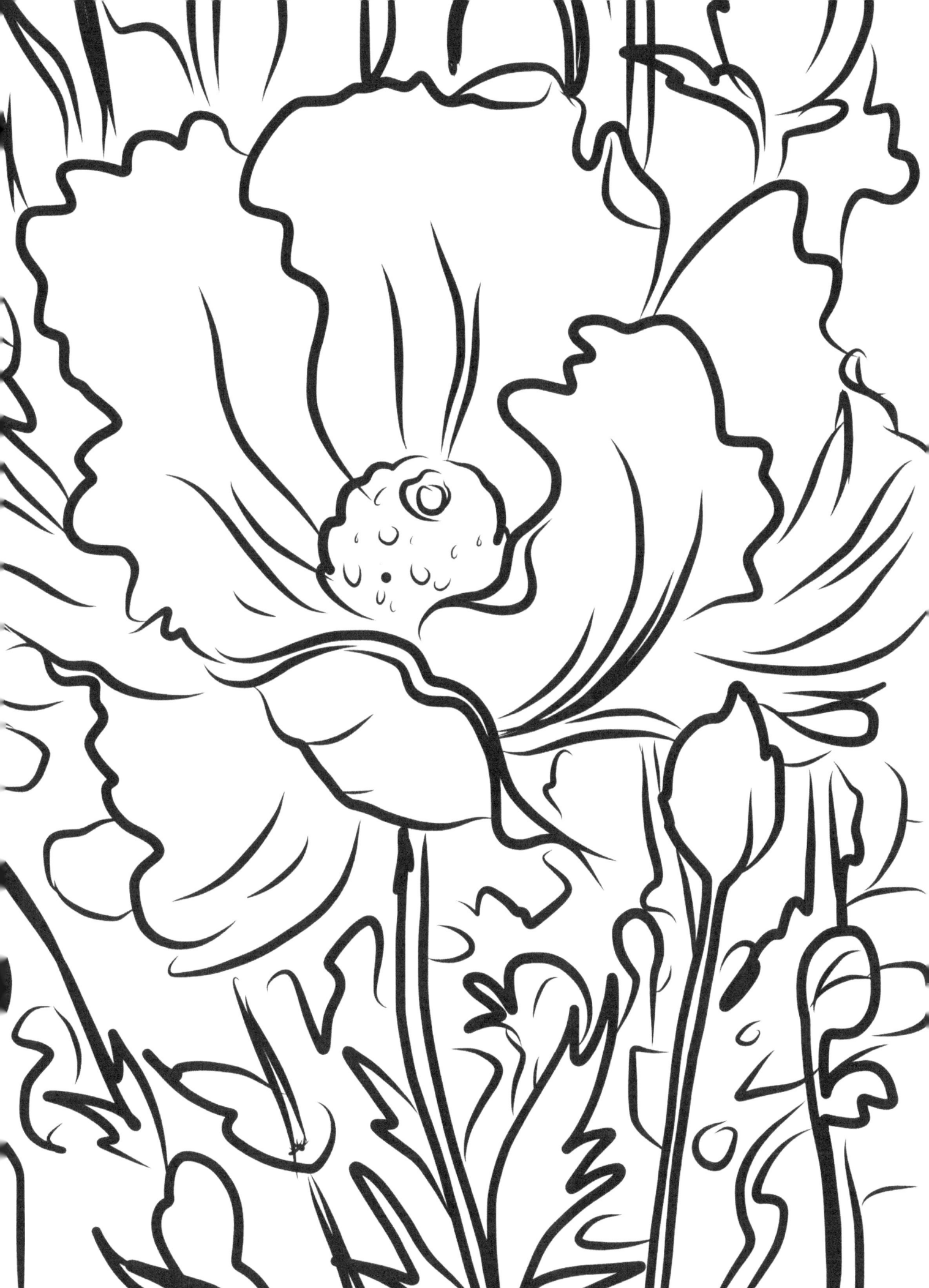

To the Edge of Eternity

When you look into a rose, the swirling vortex
of petals sweeps you into the centre of the
flower while the outer petals open and appear
to dissolve into space. Roses sometimes make
me think of the passage in Alice in Won-
derland where Alice falls down a seemingly
bottomless tunnel. What do they make you
think of?

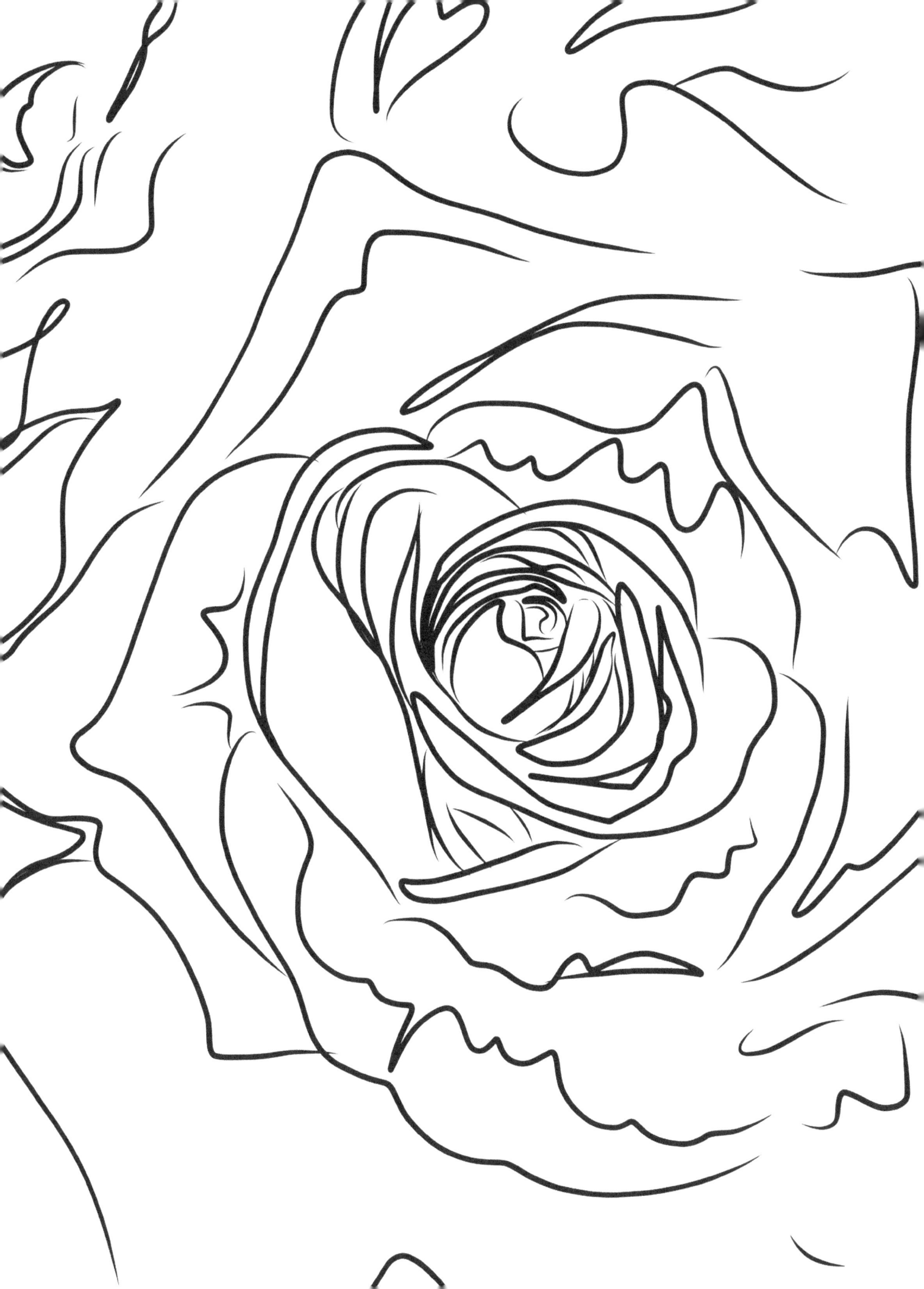

Days Like These

The bees are buzzing and the sunshine filters
through the gently flowing foliage. Every now
and again a current of air lifts the petals and
cools the warmth of the day. Birds are singing
and the garden scents drift intoxicatingly. If
only there were more days like these, moments
of intense beauty when time seems to stand
still.

If every day were perfect we would soon take
them for granted instead of accepting them
for what they are, namely simple gifts from
God. Every day brings fresh opportunities
to find and savor these moments of wonder
that constantly surround us. Have you found
yours today?

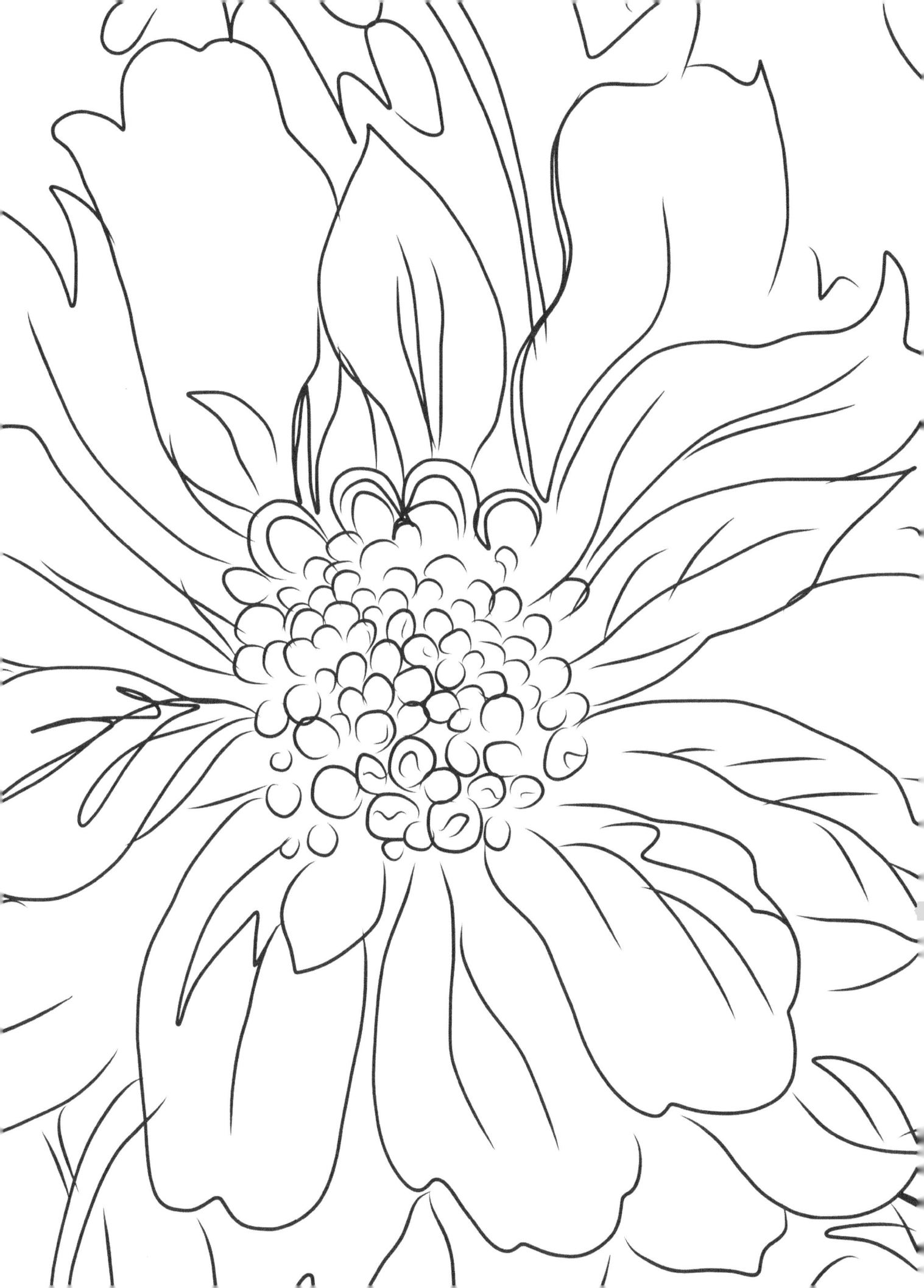

Secret Love

By its very nature, love has to make itself
known; a love that is secret cannot suffer
rejection or enjoy acceptance; but there is a
growing time for love, when the realization
of love rises in a heart, growing stronger until
that beautiful day comes and all is in the open.

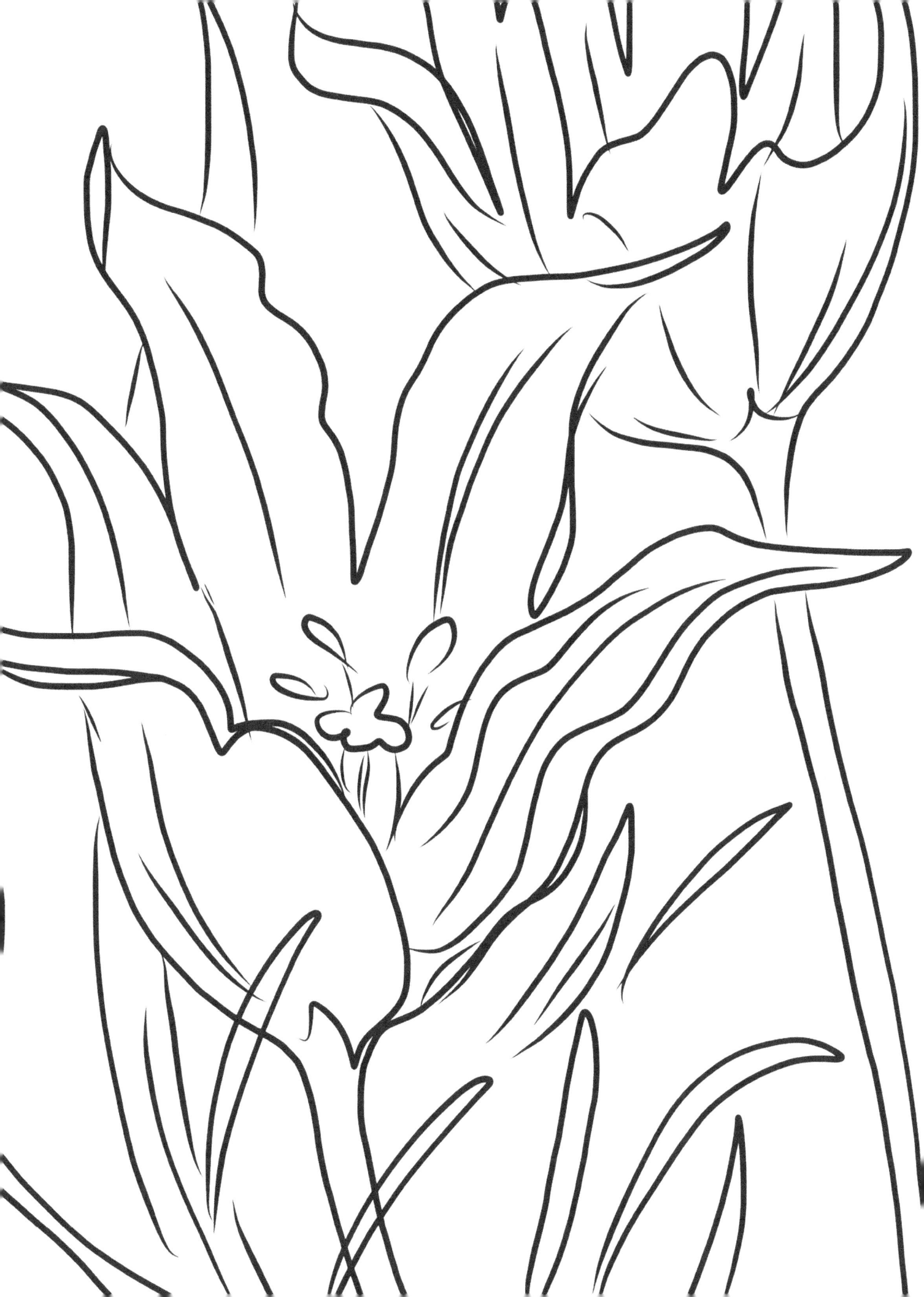

Sweet Dreams

One day I set up my easel amongst the flowers and I was drawn to this particular poppy
because of its delicate coloring and the way
the salmon pink petals harmonized with the
surrounding foliage. The softness and free
flowing brushwork of the piece led me to the
title "Sweet Dreams".

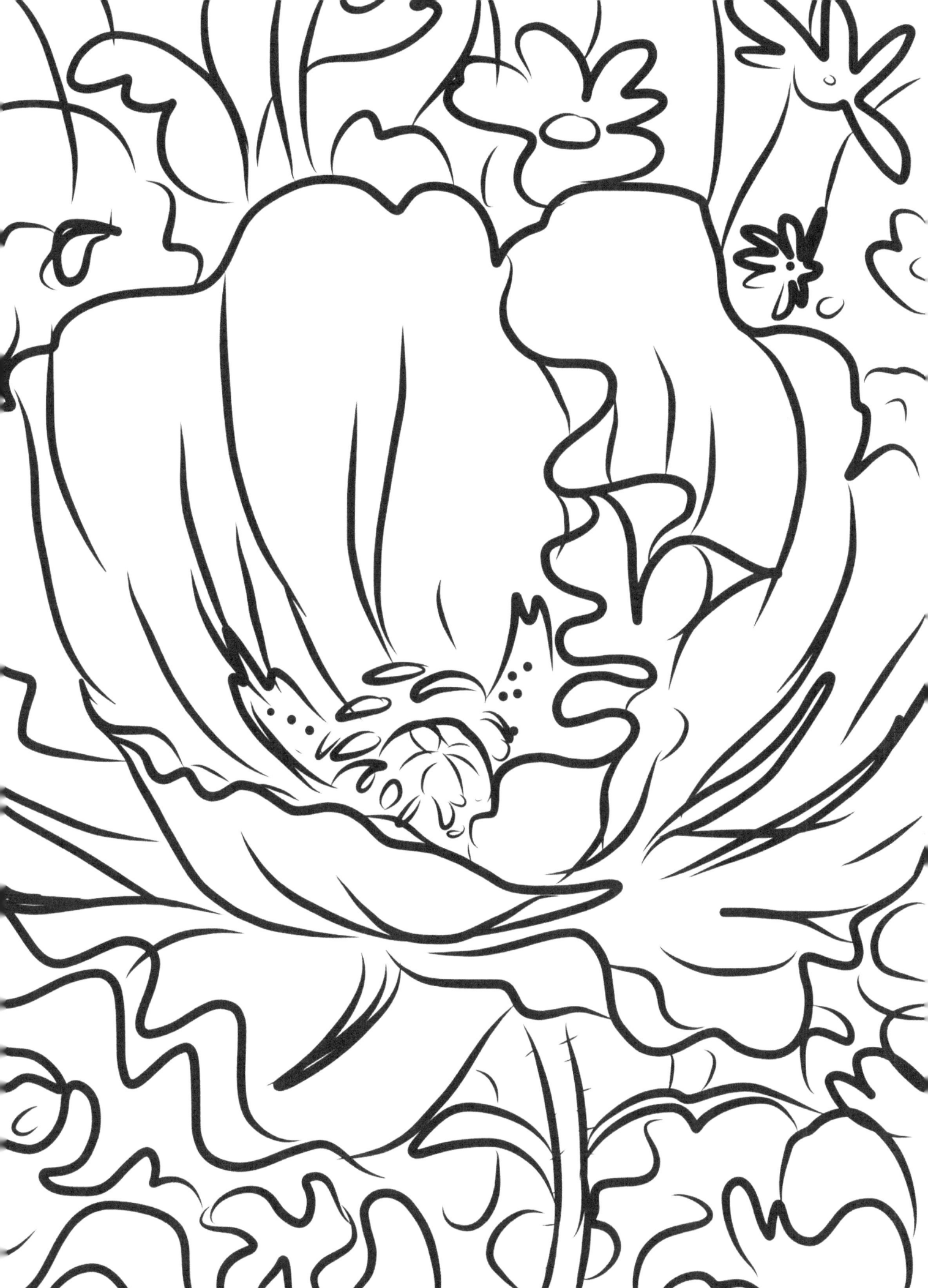

Wings of Love

I was painting one day by an old water mill,
many years ago in the Himalayan Mountains.
While I worked an old schoolteacher ap-
proached me and talked enthusiastically about
books of poetry and literature. It turned out
that he was a fan of Shakespeare and when
I asked him if he had ever been to Stratford
Upon Avon, he replied wistfully that he was
able to travel only in his dreams. I have often
thought that perhaps the Stratford he traveled
to in his mind was in some ways more real
than the actual place. Such is the power of
imagination. Let it take flight!

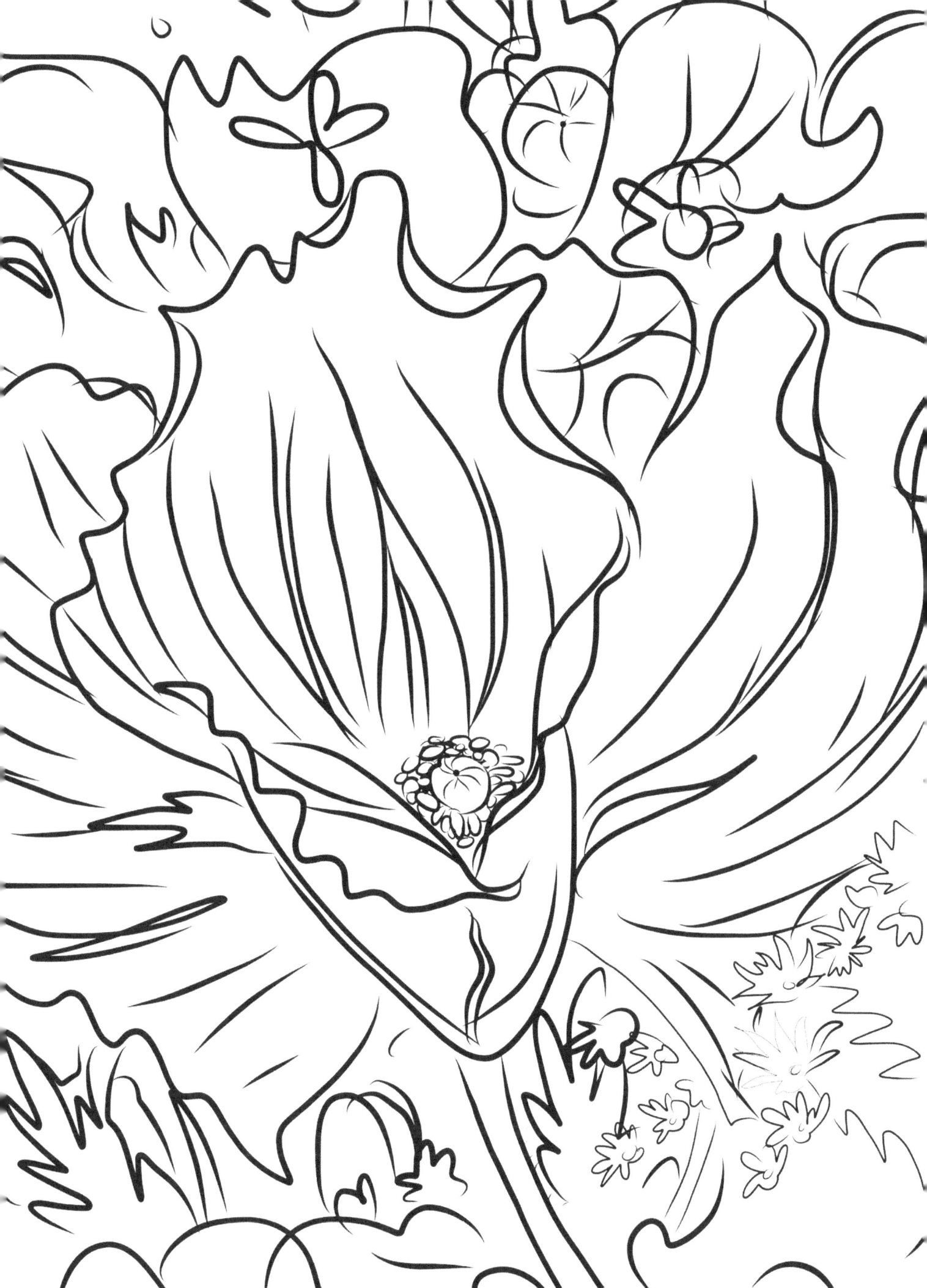

Count Your Blessings

Life is a gift and so are the simple pleasures
that are extravagantly ours every day: the sky
above our heads, the smell of the morning air
as it brushes our cheek; the conversation of
friends or the laugh of a child; the memories
we carry with us and the hopes we have for
tomorrow.

There is an old song we used to sing in Sun-
day School, perhaps you know it. "Count your
blessings, name them one by one, then you'll
be amazed at what the Lord has done." What
gift has been bestowed upon you today? You
may only see problems, but look closer, listen
more attentively, because you could soon be
unwrapping surprising treasures.

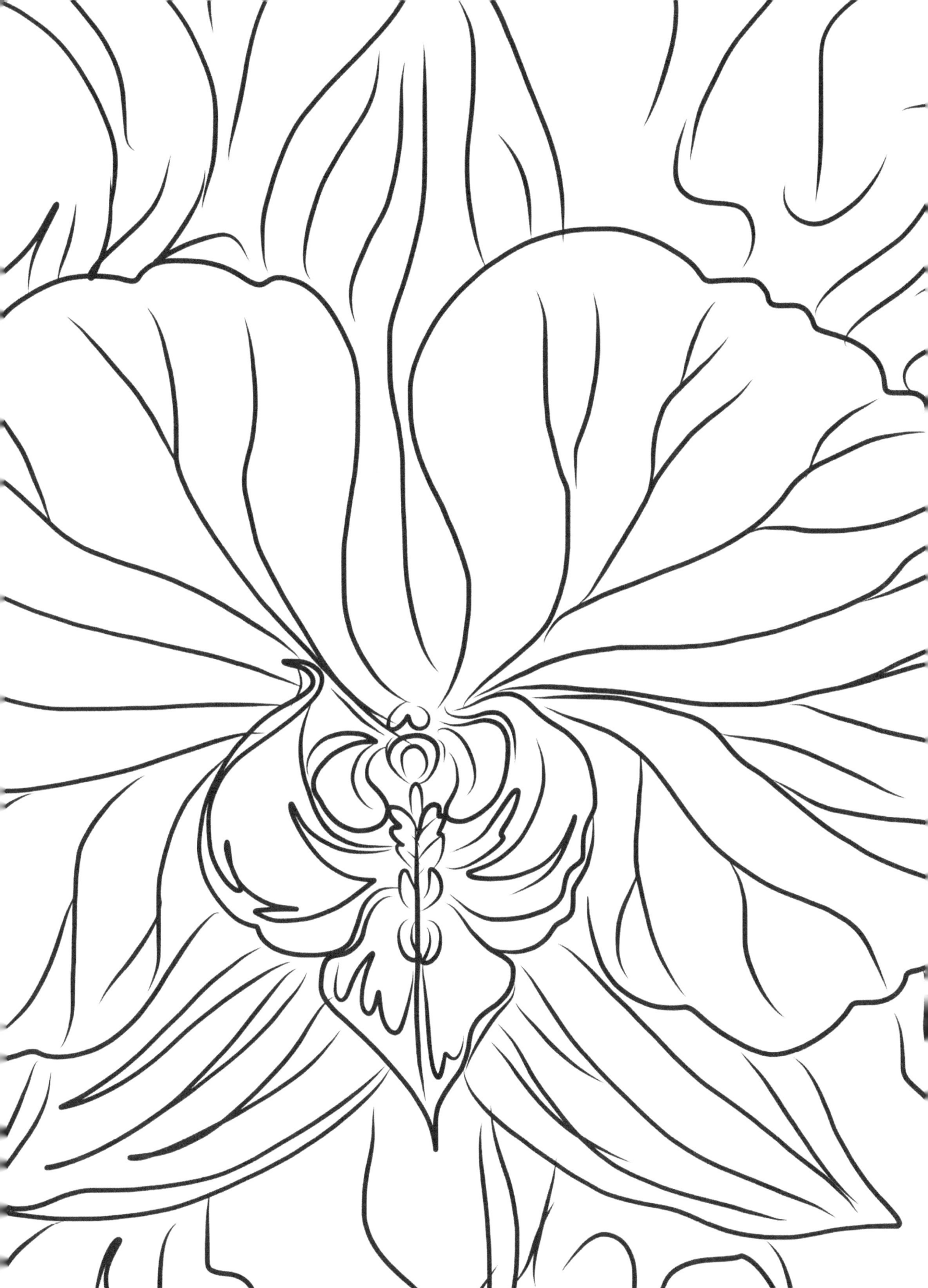

Forever

I once heard a preacher say that eternity was a
very long time and I could never understand
that, because surely eternity is no time at all.
Eternity happens when time ends and is something beyond our experience. But in another
sense eternity is now, right here in the present
moment. Life's greatest gift.

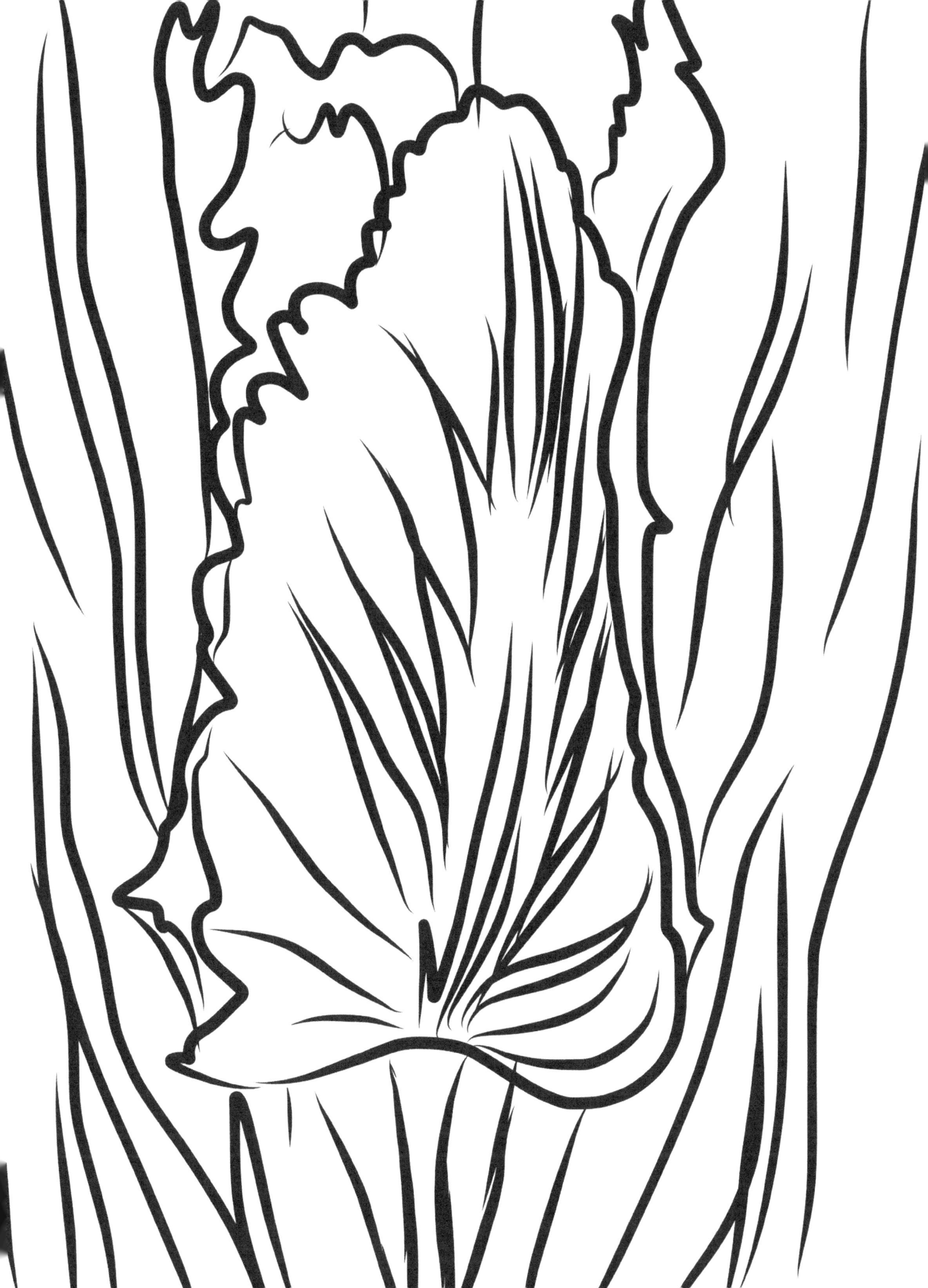

Smallest of Dreams

There are times when the day with all its reality seeks to erase the half remembered reveries
of the night. In such moments, how exquisite
are those fragments even of the smallest of
dreams.

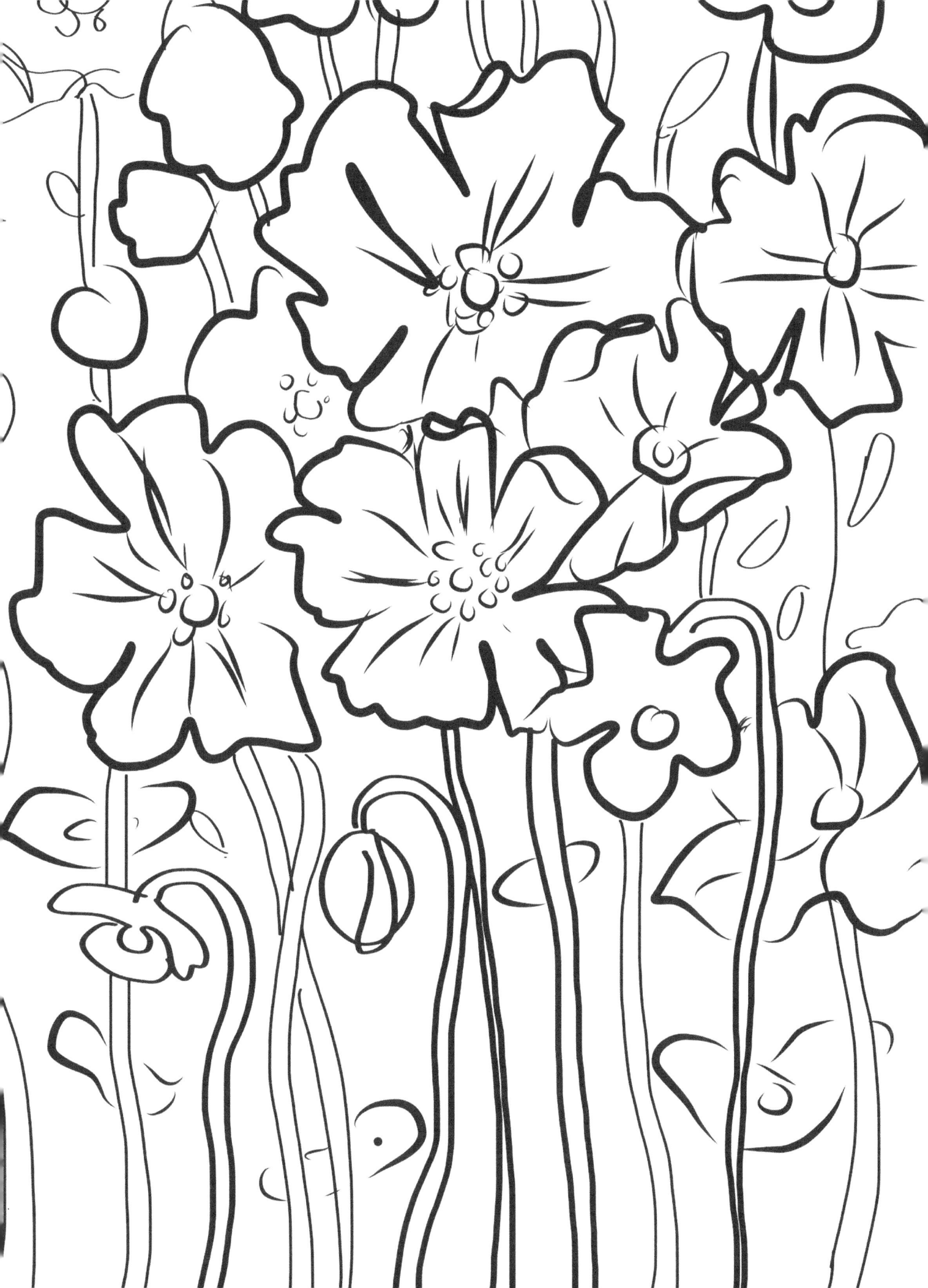

Thistle

Cultivated flowers make for great subjects, but
there is something about the wild flower that
speaks deeply. The thistles that are abundant
in England during the summer attract a wide
variety of insects, including one of my favorite,
the six spot burnet moth. Check out the six
spots on its wings.

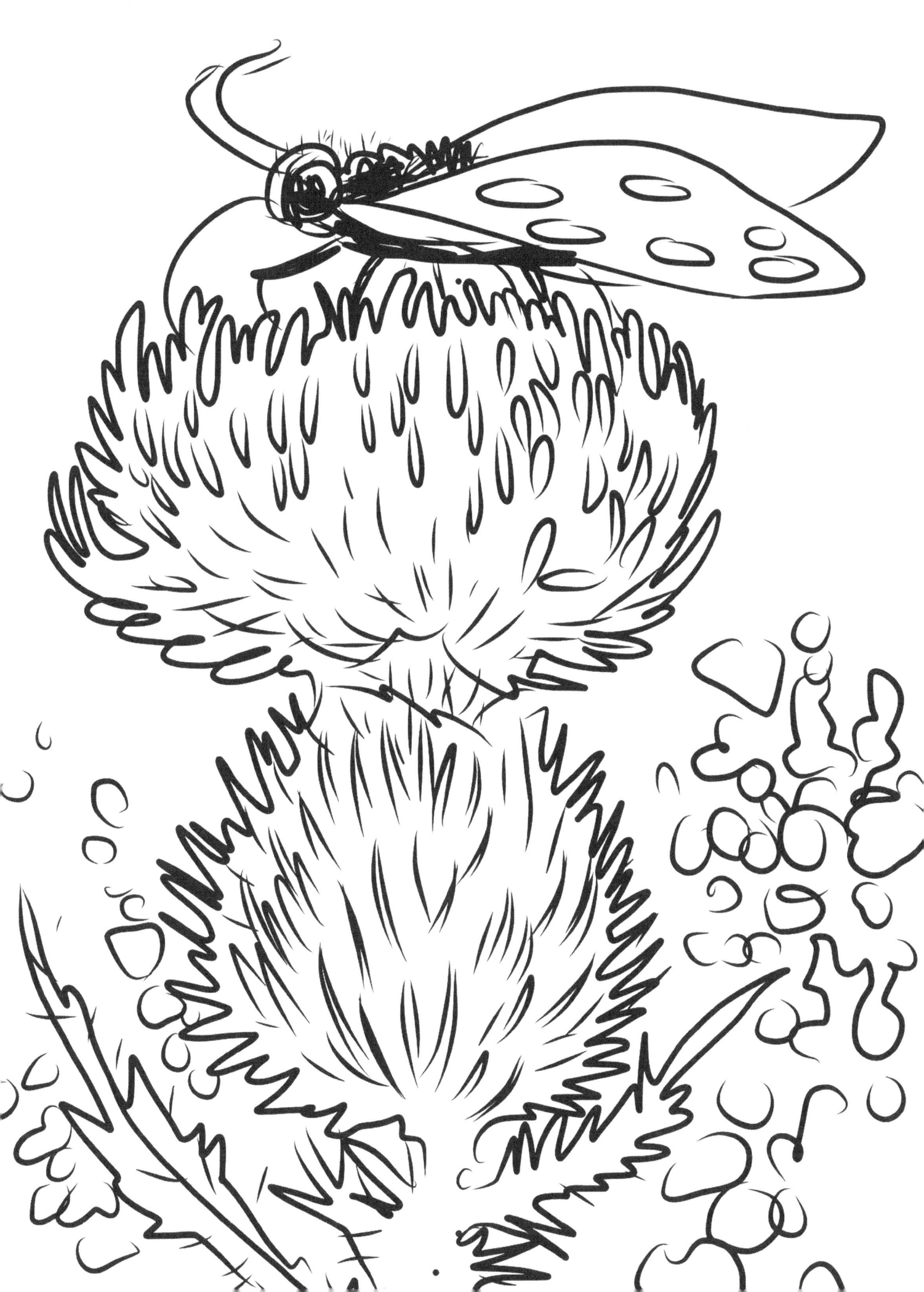

Amarylis

We try to plant a few amaryllis bulbs every
year and although it's a bit of a task, they richly reward the effort.

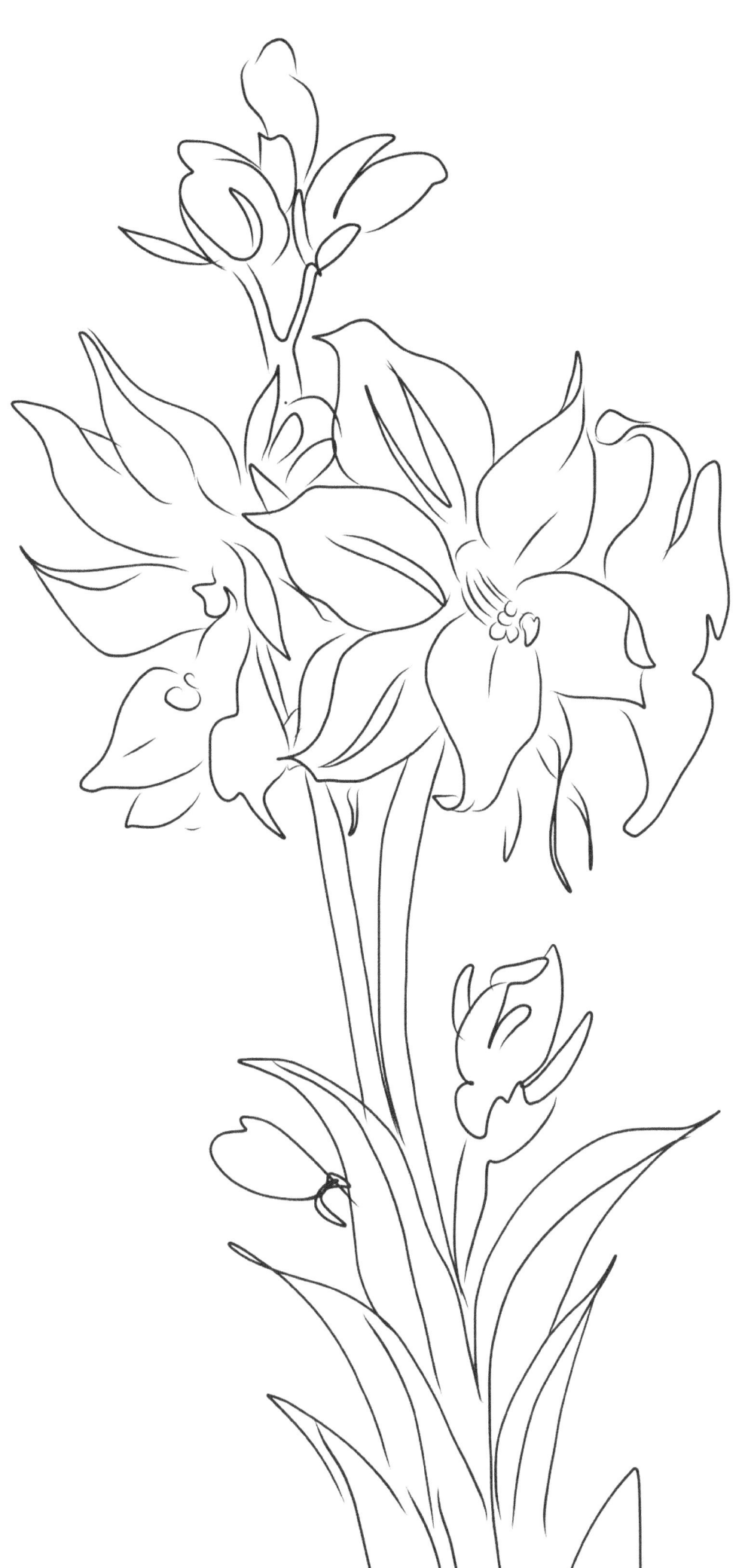

Angels Among us

I painted this for a dear friend who's wife was
battling brain cancer. It depicts the suffering
soul surrounded by a celestial army of loving
supporters, these are the friends, the nurses,
the doctors and family who circle the ailing
loved one in their time of need.

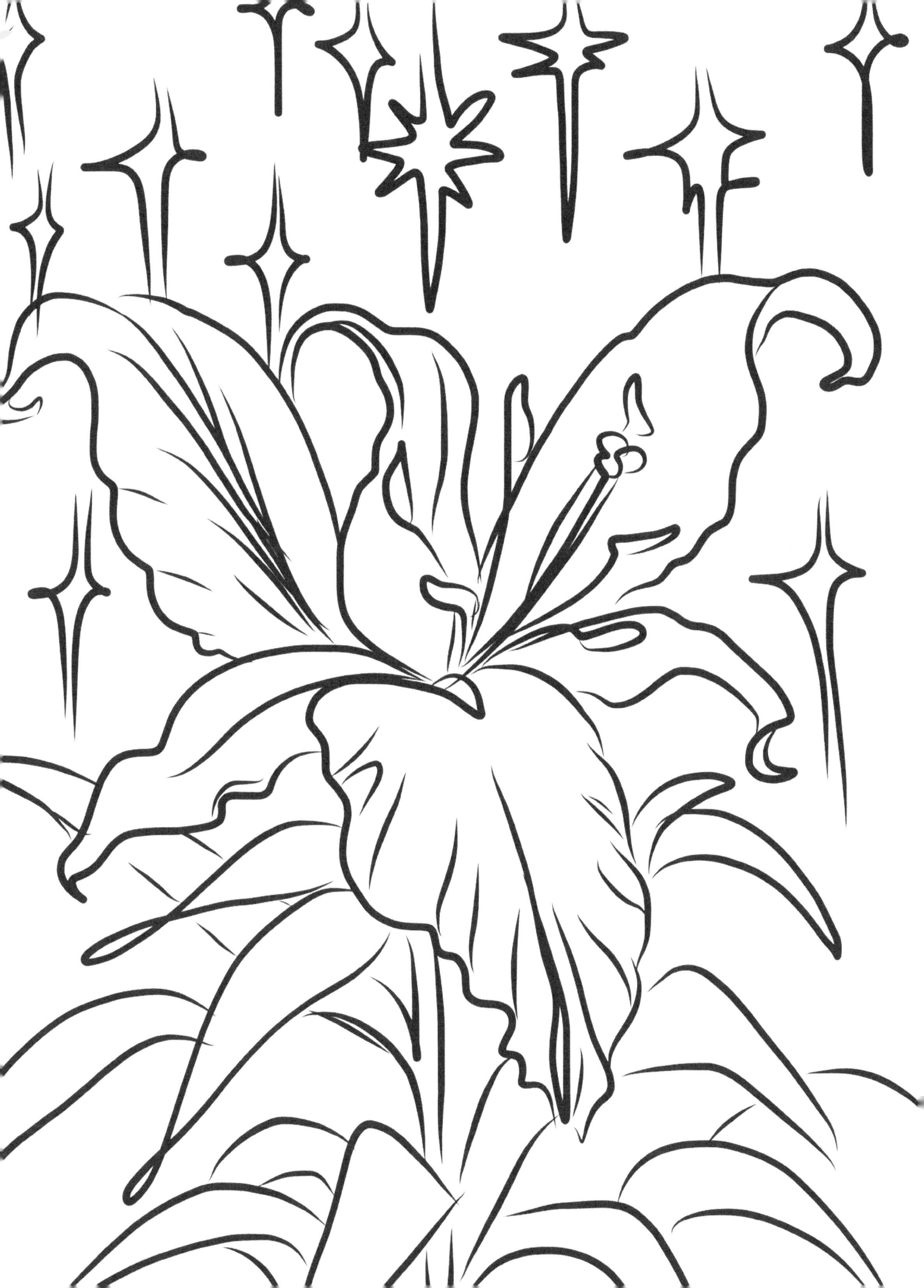

Spellbound

Sunflowers have intriguing personalities,
perhaps more so than other flowers. It could
be something to do with their size, or perhaps
because they usually grow together in a community. Either way, walking among mature
sunflowers as they tower above you and gazing
at their radiant features is a feast for the eyes
and senses.

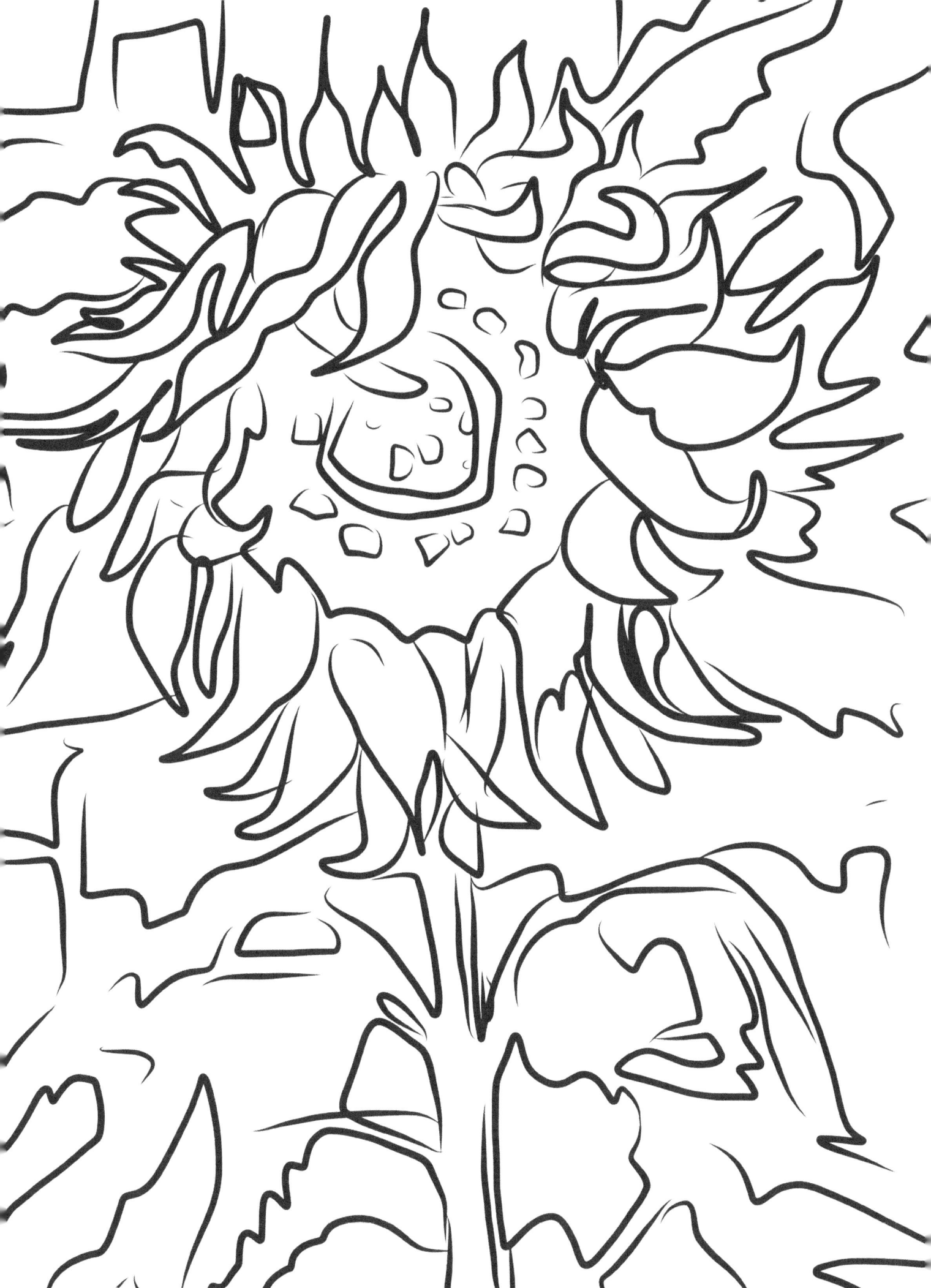

Anthurium

The anthurium grows in tropical climates and
makes a beautiful splash of love heart red in
the forest.

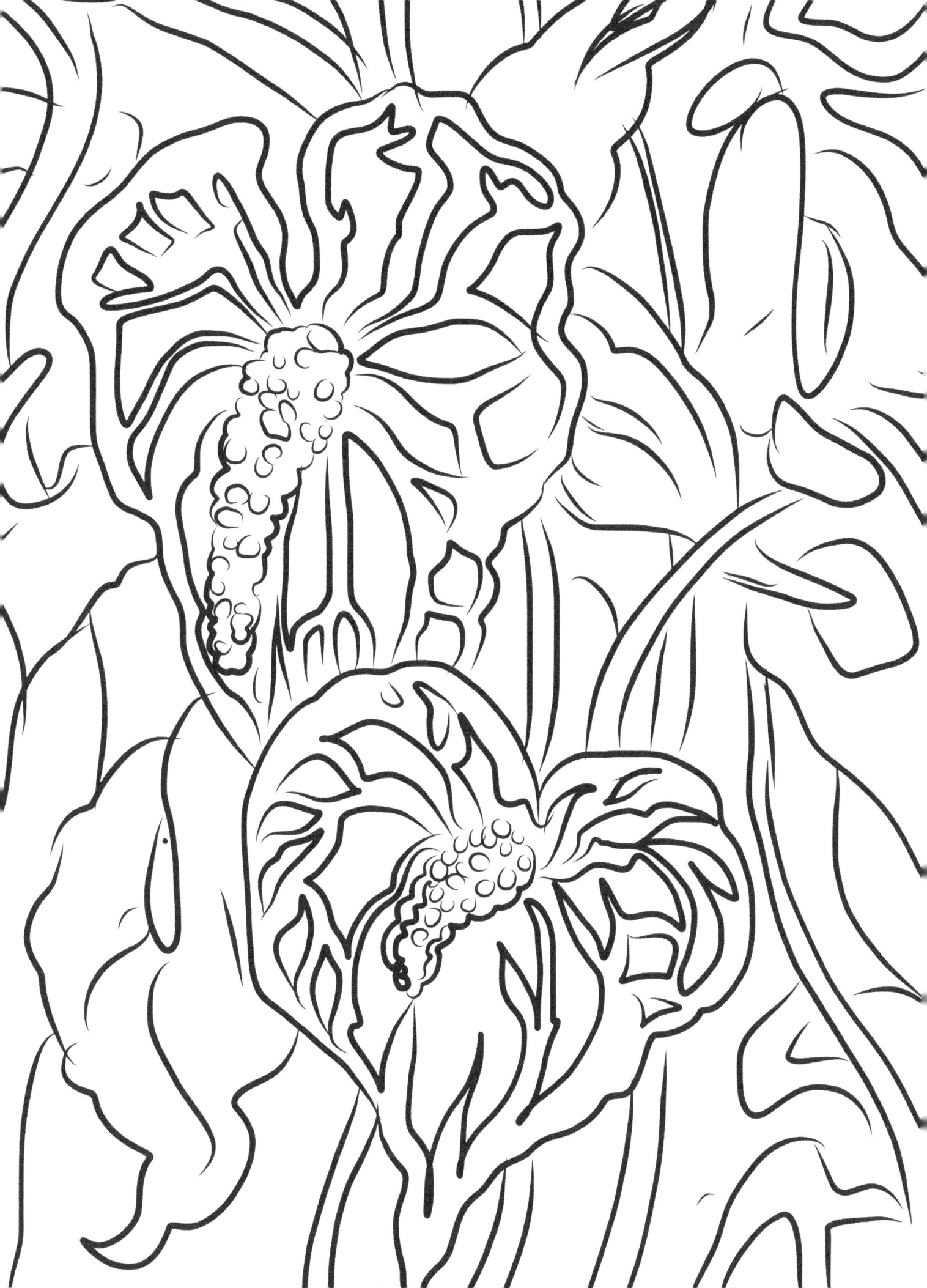

Adoration

Adoration is a special kind of love, a tender love, a devotional love. It makes those close to us feel more than special, it affirms and empowers them. It also has a tendency to work two ways - try loving devotedly and feel the difference!

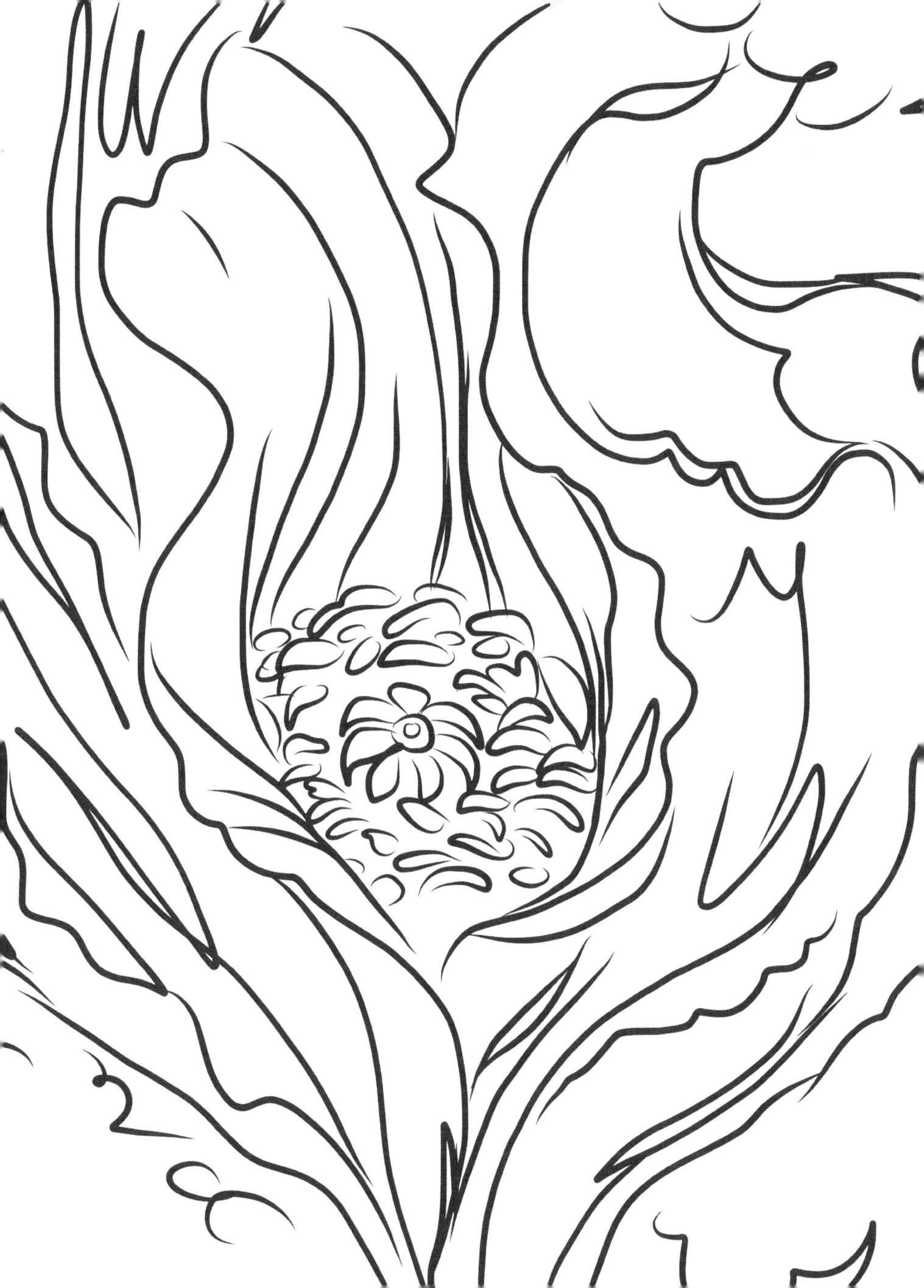

Bird of Paradise

Named after the exotic birds of dazzling color and exotic plumage. The Strelitzia brings a little flash of Paradise into the here and now with it's complimentary crown of blue, orange and gold.

This image also won an award. The NALED (National Association of Limited Edition Dealers) 2004 Print of the year.

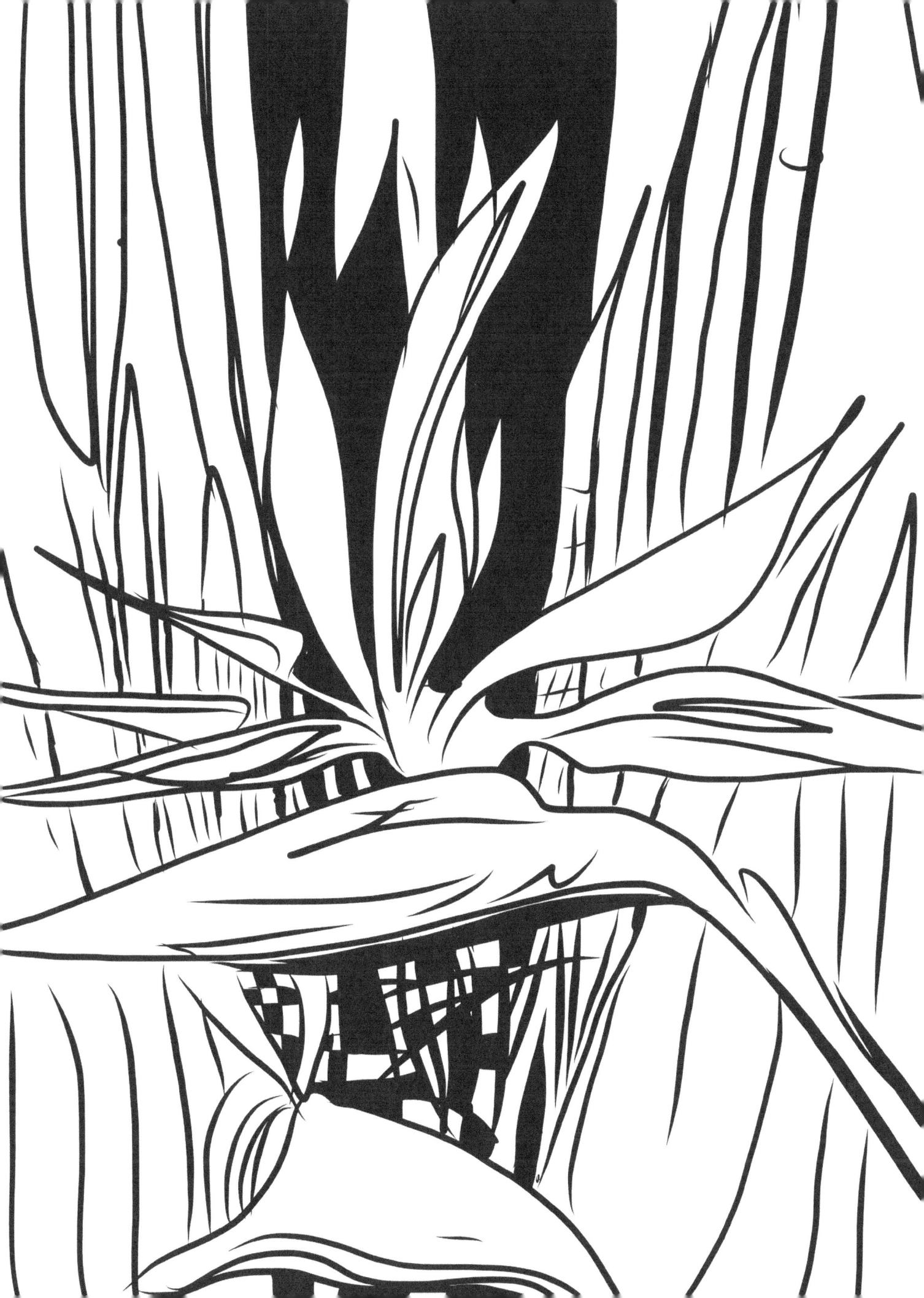

We Believe

To believe, to hold a truth so dearly and with
such deep conviction that it changes the way
we live is a powerful thing. But when belief
is shared and we can say: "We believe," the
possibilities that open to such a consensus are
without limit.

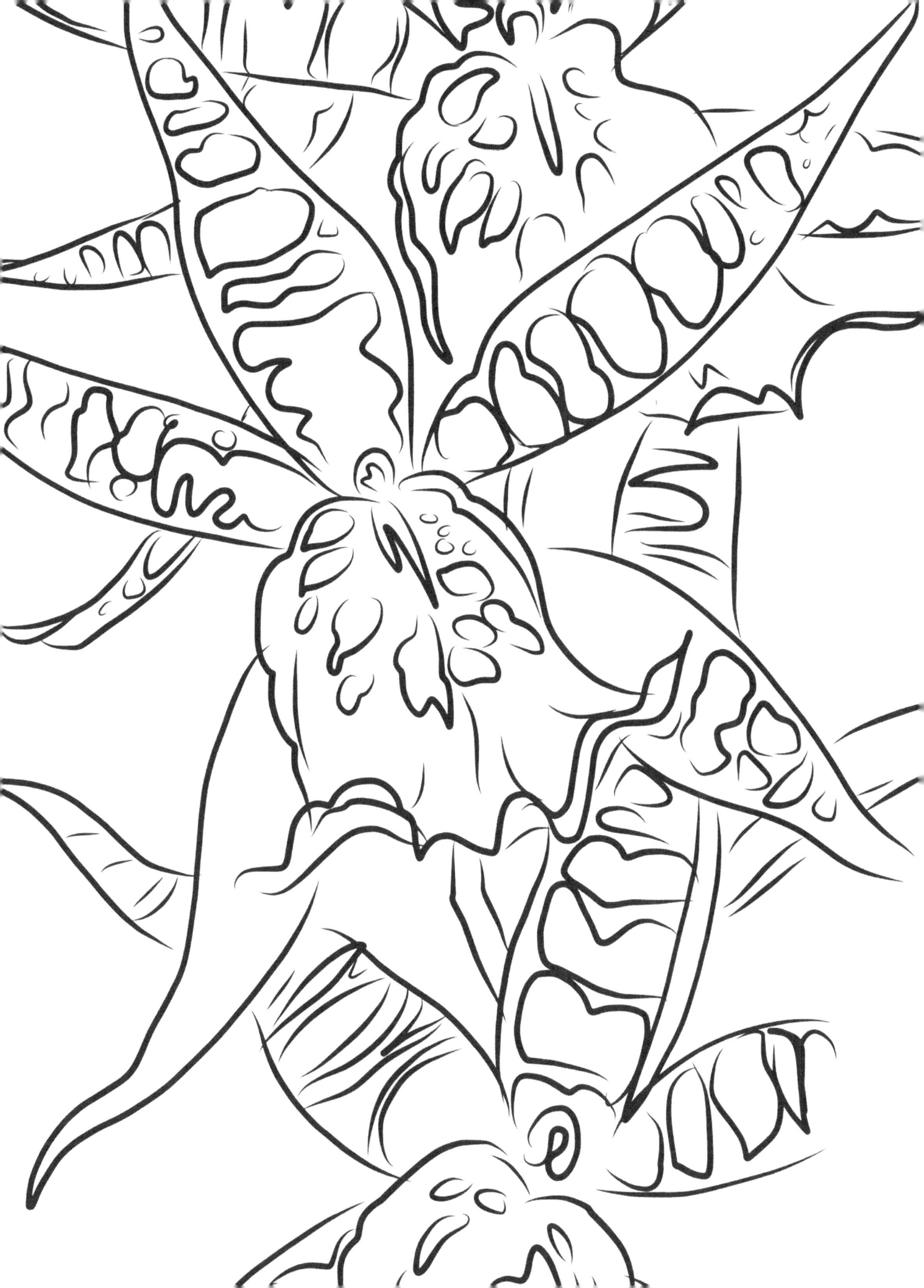

Daisy

Flowers are like little explosions, at least from
a distance. From closer in, their explosive
nature becomes more significant.

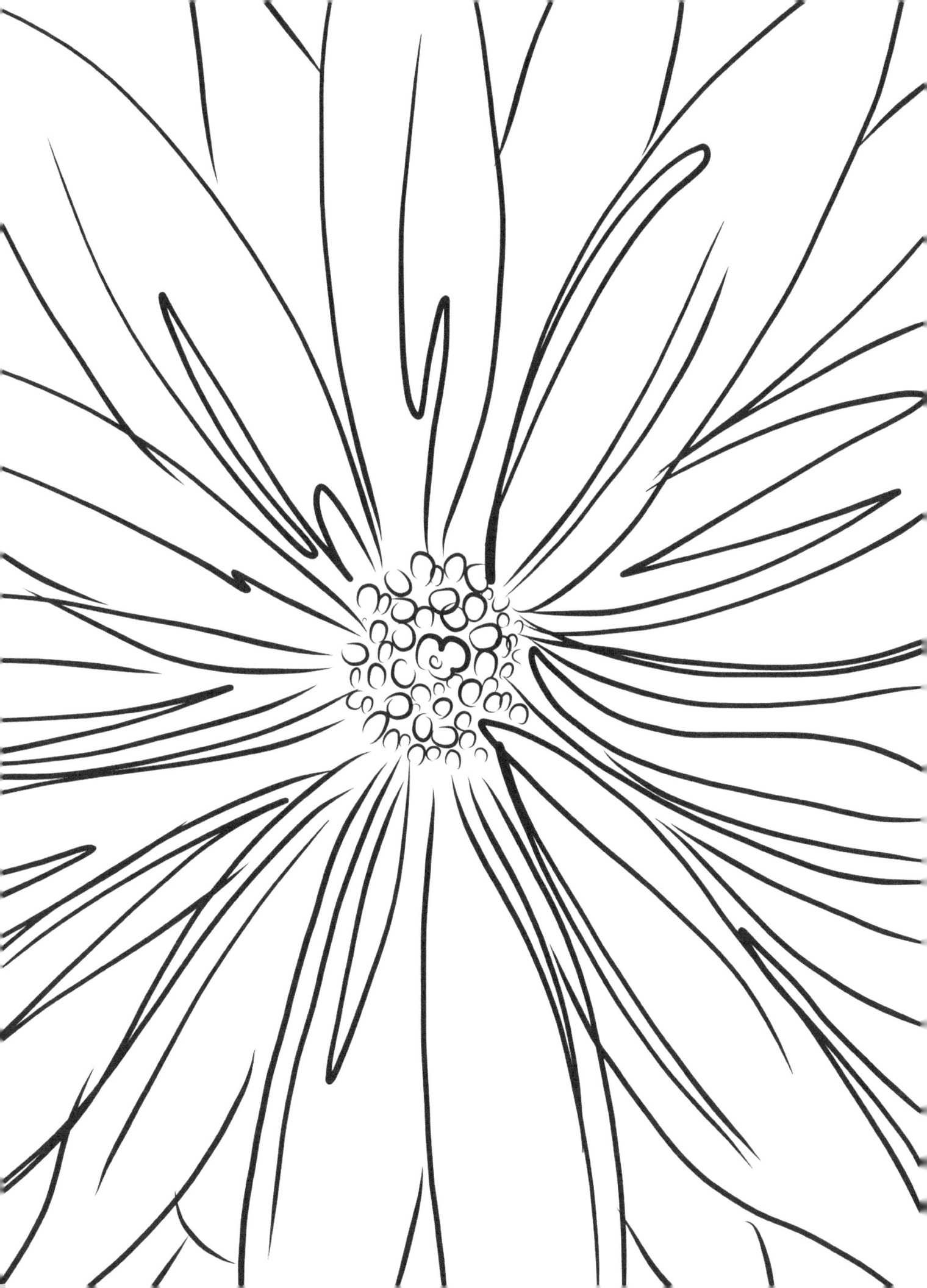

Kiss the Sky

I called this one, Kiss the Sky for obvious rea-
sons, But now it's in black and white you can
do what you want with it. Make it your own.

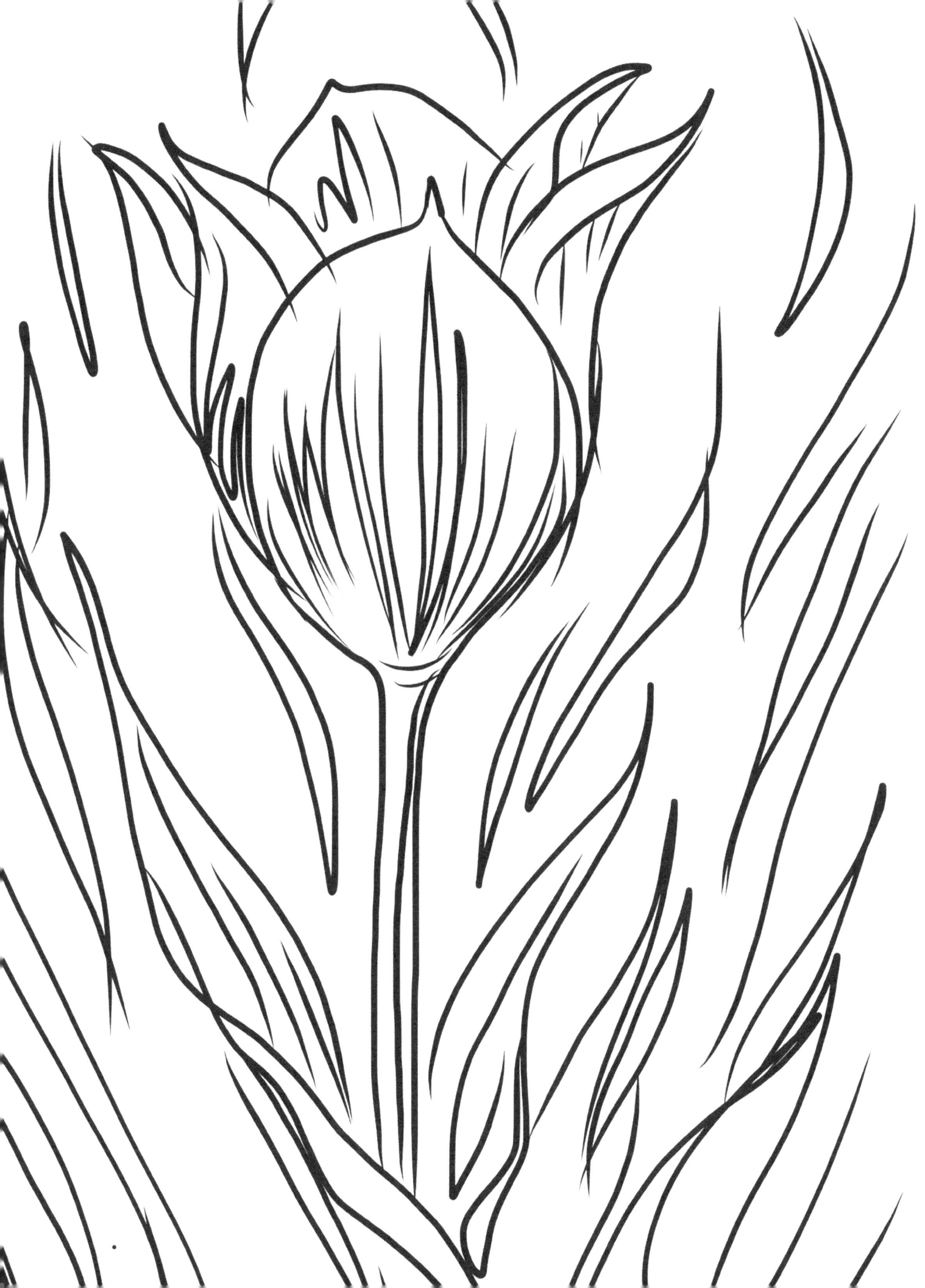

Let My Words be Few

There are times when our words can express
so much, but we can over use our verbal facil-
ity, I remember reading the famous Victorian
Theologian CH Spurgeon once and he passed
on this advice to his students: "God deliver me
from the gift of being able to say nothing at
great length". Sometimes, it is best that words
should cease and we should instead simply
bow in awe before eternity.

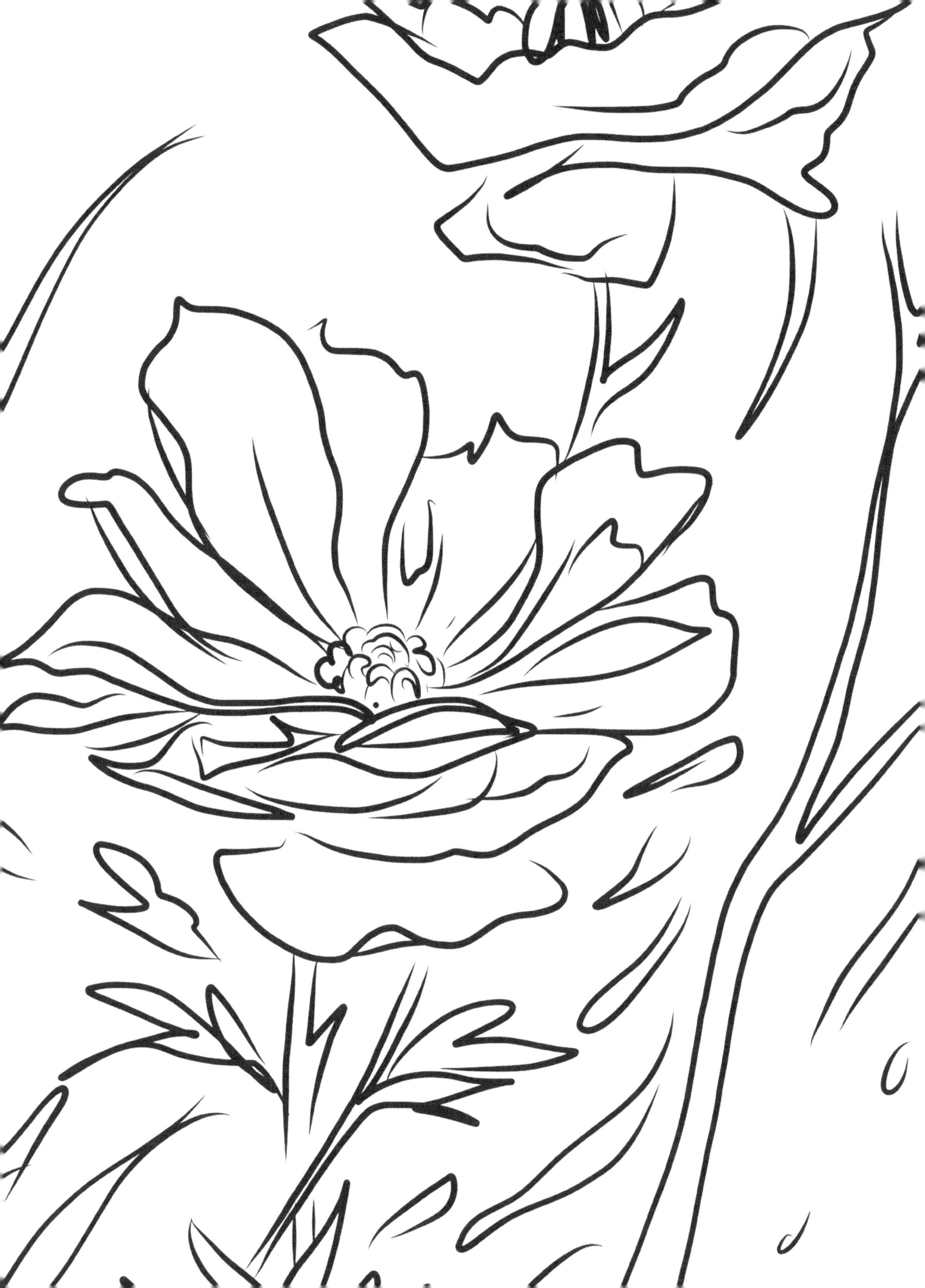

Eternity

Every year an elegant display of tulips grows
just outside my studio window. I watch them
from the earliest spring when the first tender shoots push out towards the light right
through to the warm summer evenings when
one by one the brilliant red petals begin to fall.
They create a poignant little sideshow as they
bob in the wind and I find I appreciate whatever stage they are at, knowing that even in
winter when there is no sign of them above
ground, that each stage of life, for them as for
us, is equally important, equally significant.

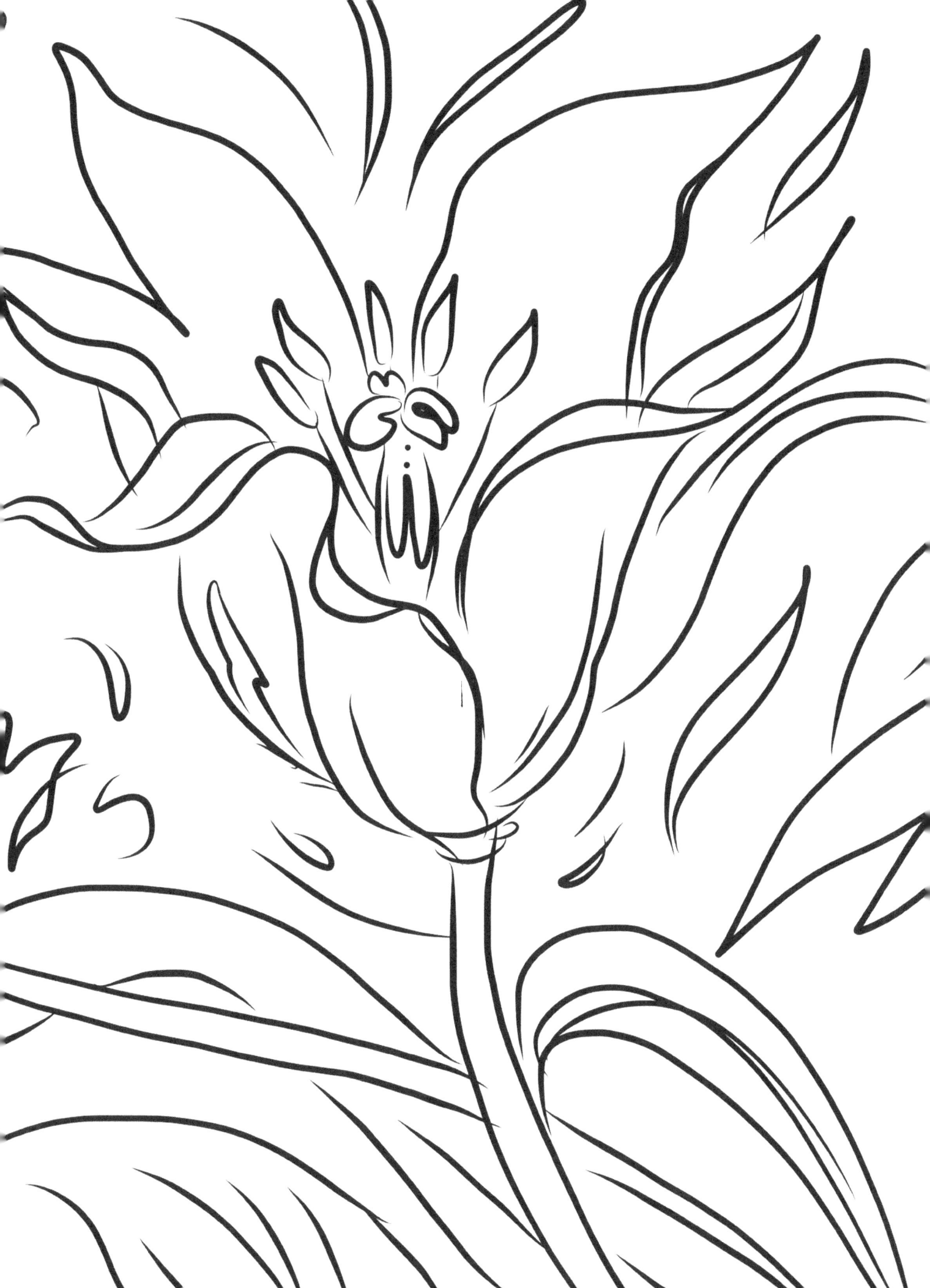

Bells

If the garden was an orchestra, these little
fuchsia's would be in the percussion section,
awaiting their turn to contribute melodic
chimes to the sweeping melody of the day.

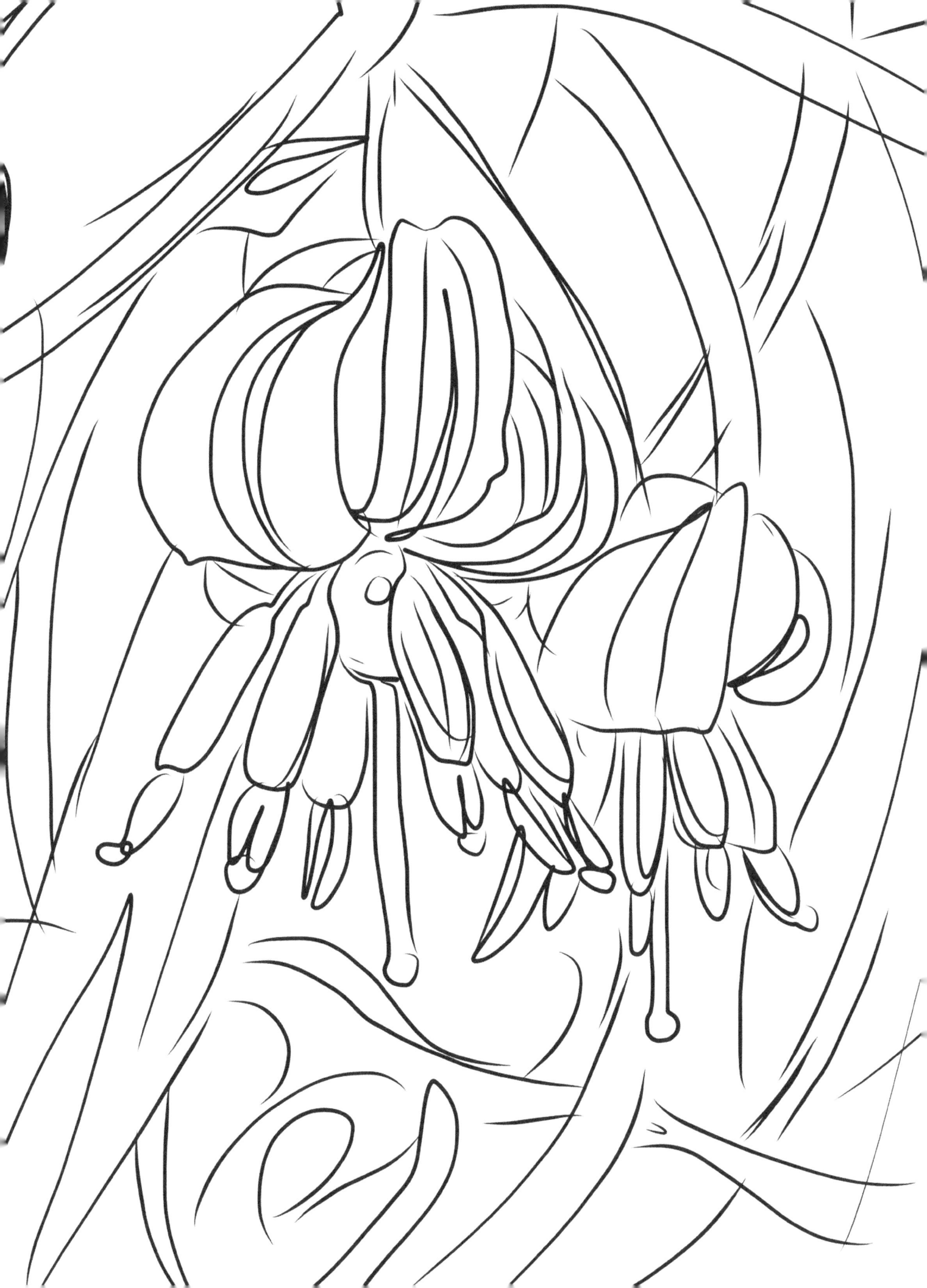

Empress

Most of the year the iris lies dormant, taking
up valuable space in the garden, sometimes it
seems hardly worth keeping. But in early summer, when the spiked buds open into fairytale
castles that dance on the breeze, all is forgiv-
en, as this queen of flowers flourishes like an
empress.

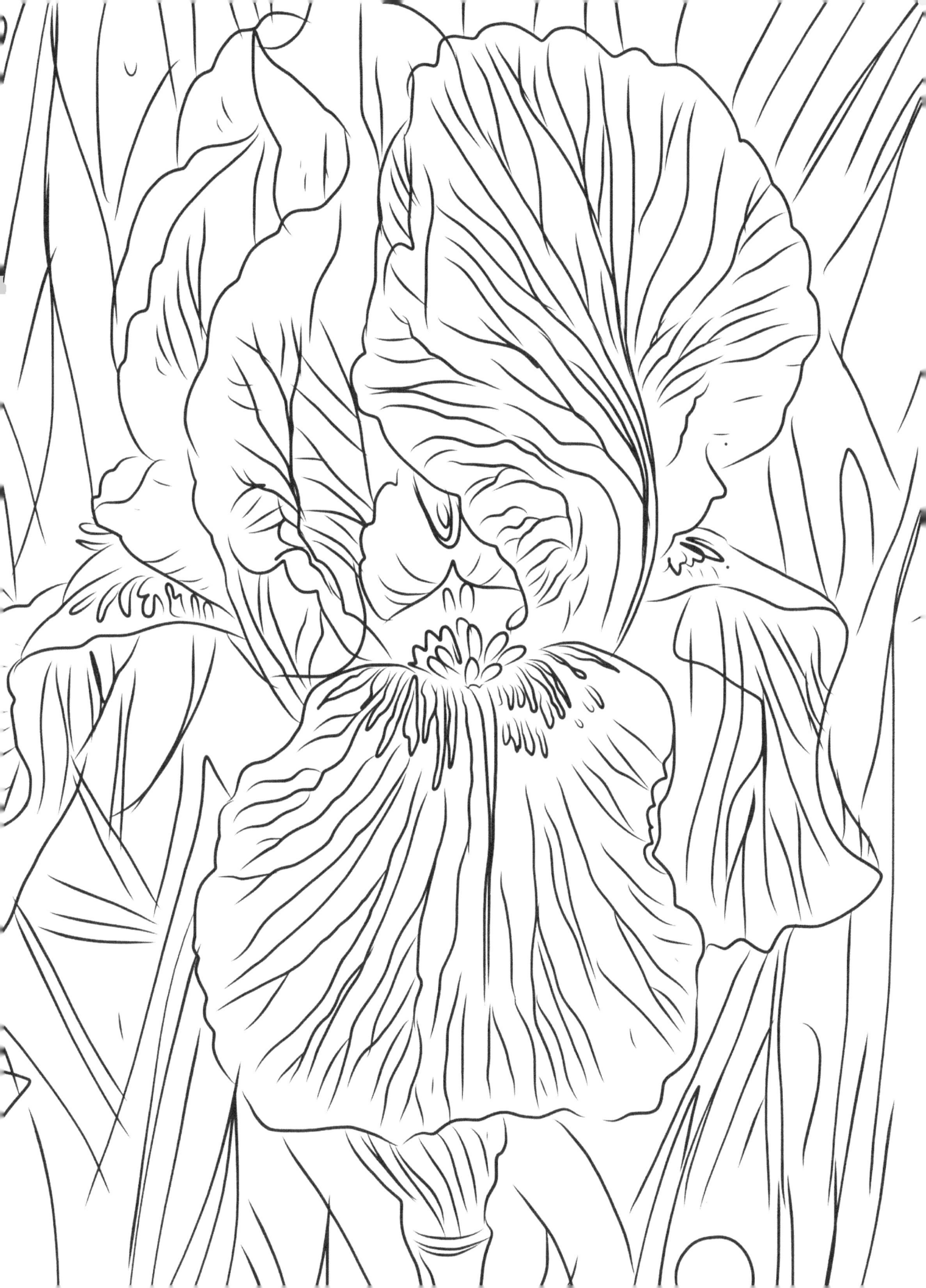

Just the Way You Are

I love you…just the way you are! Doesn't it
make you feel wonderful when someone close
says that, and means it? We all want to change
something about ourselves, the way we look,
our feelings, our education or even our financ-
es and sometimes that all feels like hard work,
especially when our best efforts can appear
to produce so little at times. Knowing that
we are loved exactly as we are paradoxically
brings about the greatest change of all, by em-
powering us to truly be ourselves, whoever we
are, whatever our circumstances.

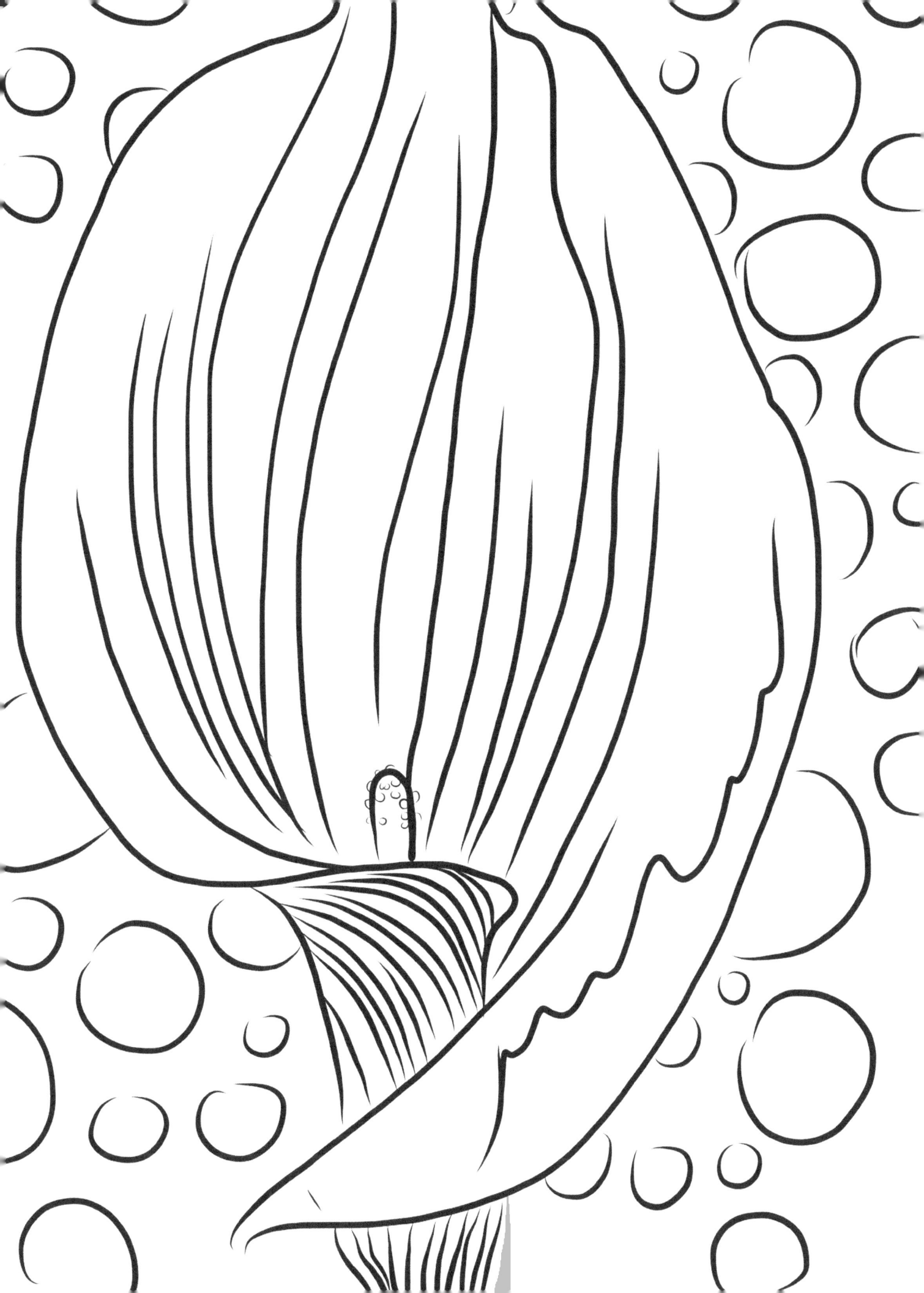

Poppies

Poppies, poppies, poppies. I have painted
them so many times and yet I still find myself
in love, head over heels with this exotic beauty.
I never fail to see something new every time I
look into their luminous gossamer petals.

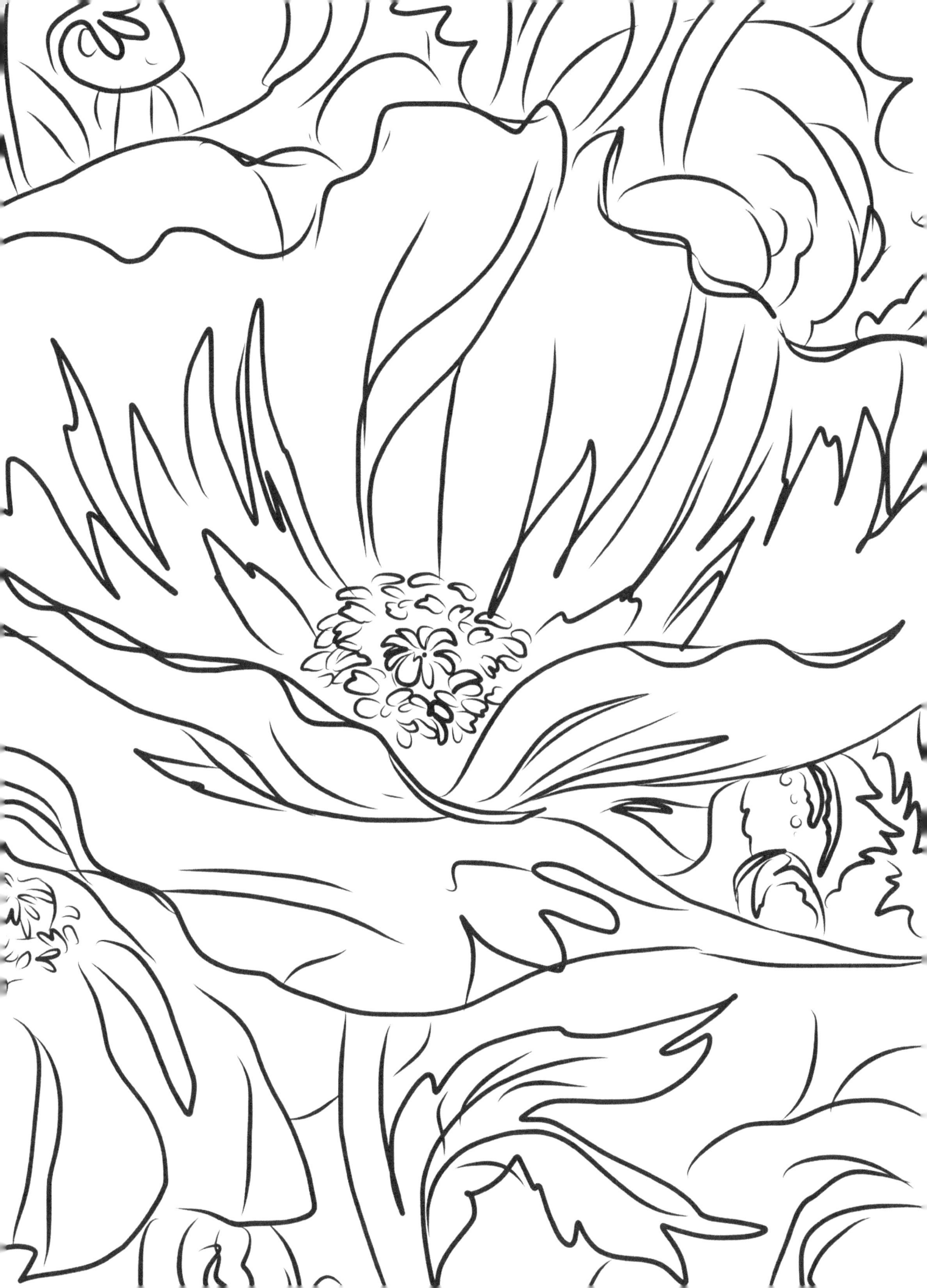

Tuscany Gold

Take me to the hills of Tuscany, where, on a
summer's evening the sound of the cicadas
gives way to the rhythmic cadence of the
crickets, and the mellow rays of the fading sun
turn the honeyed hills to gold. Take me to that
place where the earth's fertile loam has yielded
nurture and sustenance from generation to
generation and fields of amber sunflowers are
lulled to sleep under the waking stars.

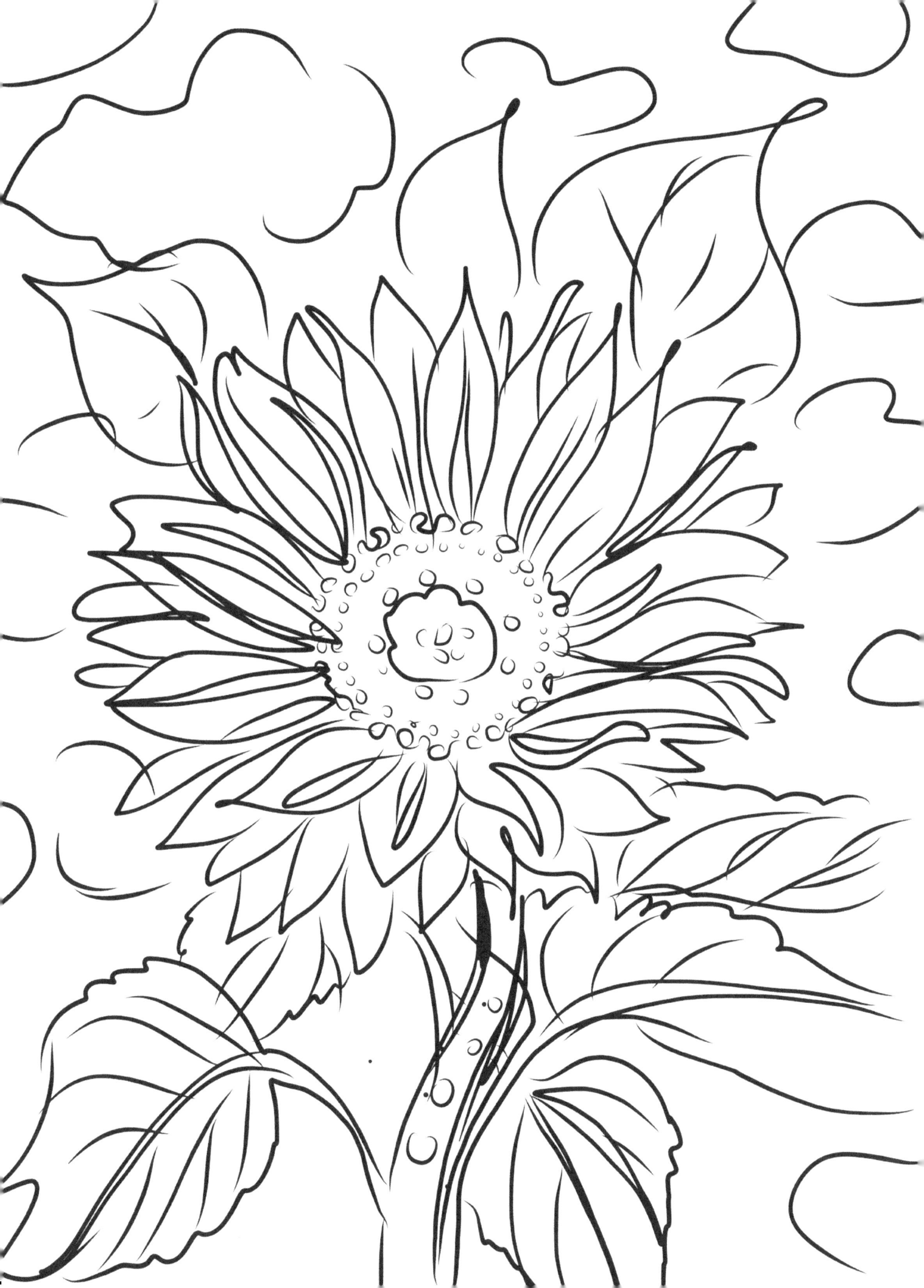

With all my Heart

Love is an interesting emotion, just when you
feel you have given your all, instead of shutting
down, your heart grows a little bigger and cre-
ates more capacity.   Love it seems is its own
medicine, the more you love the more you are
able to love.   Let us love then, but let us do it
with all, not just a part of our hearts.

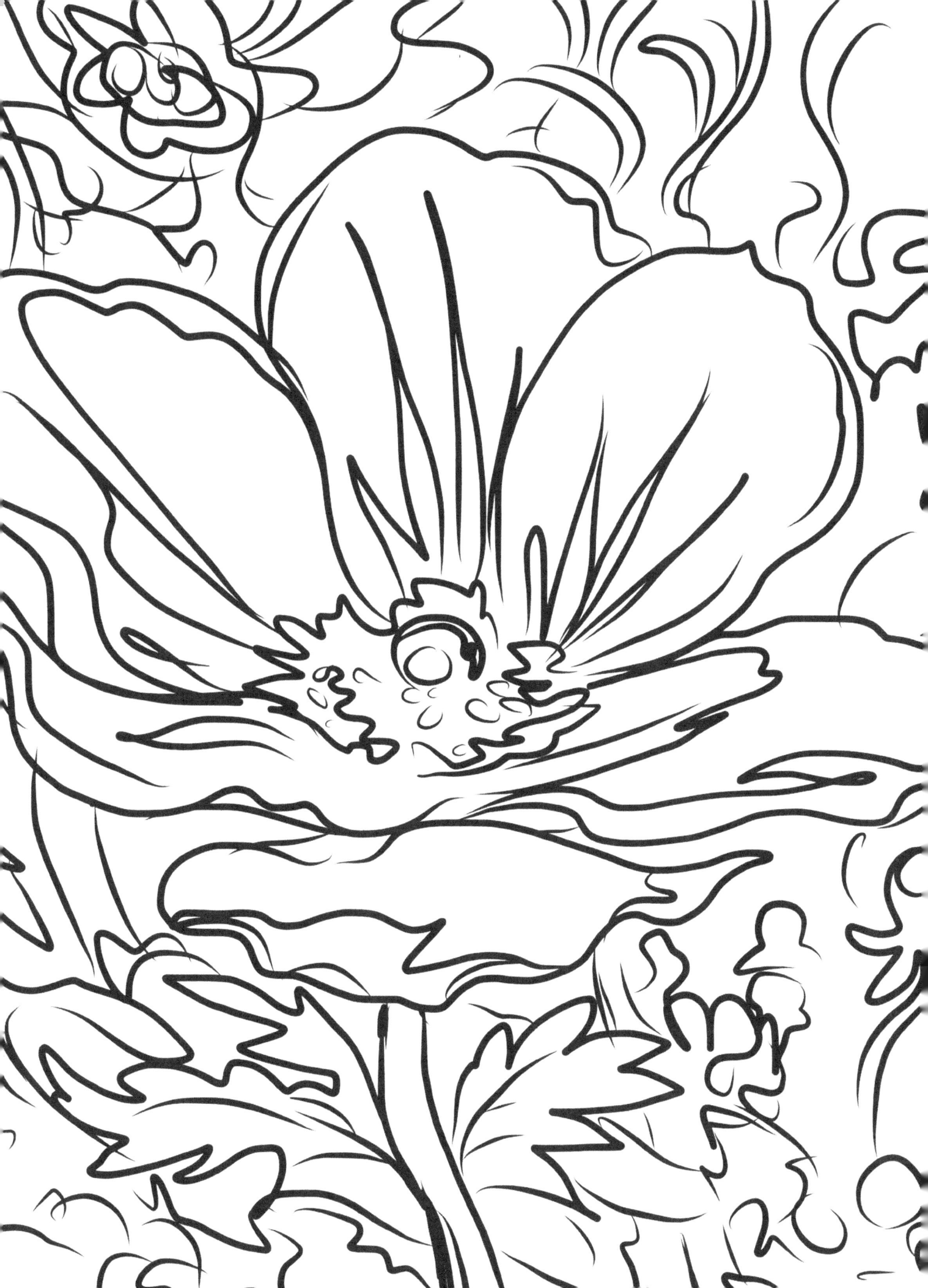

Sacred Geometry

If you stop and think about it flowers are all
about geometry. At school I was not that into
set squares and rulers, but as I have spent time
studying flowers with pencil in hand I have
learnt to appreciate those things more and
more. What do you see in this?

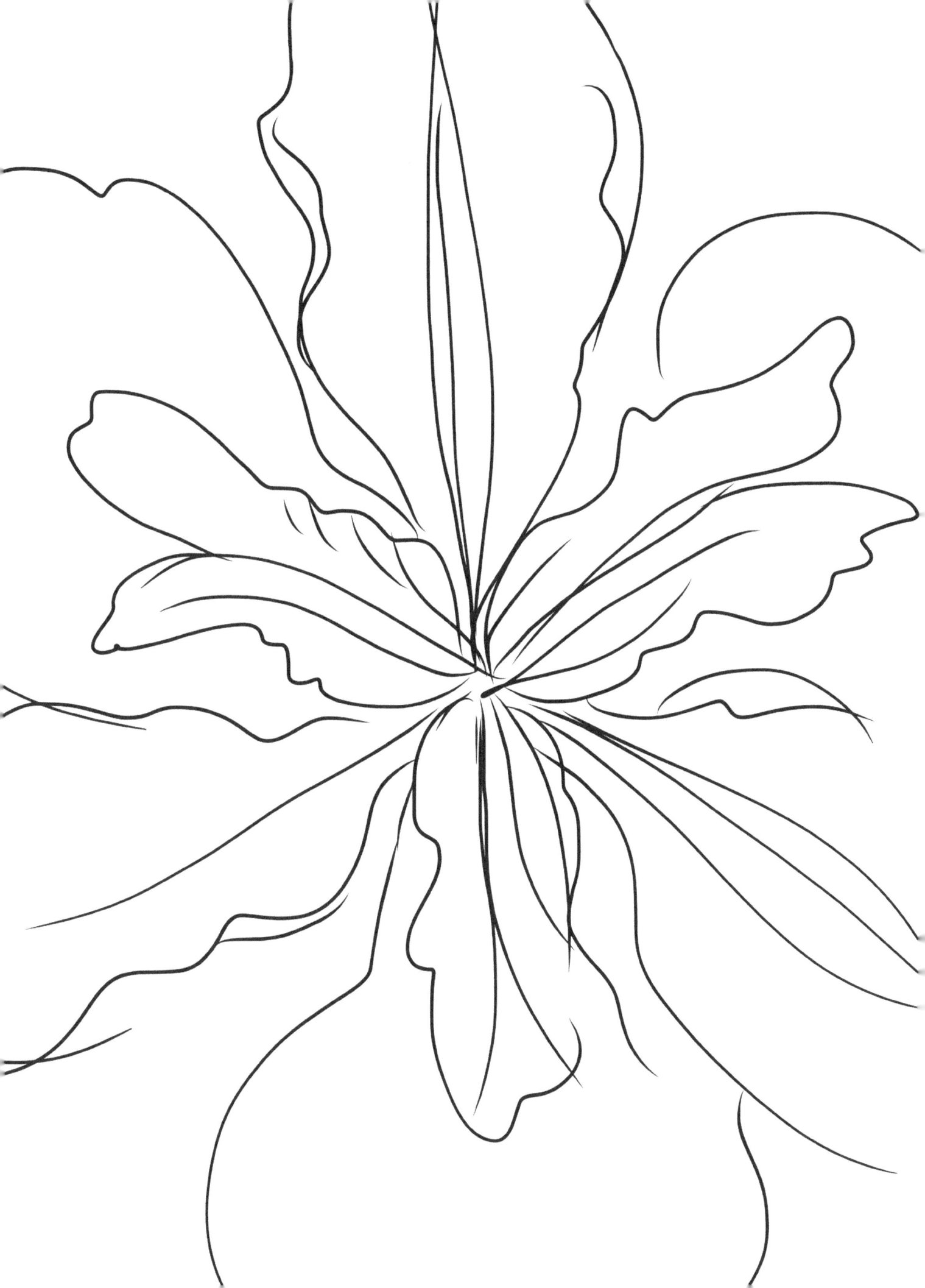

Serendipity

Don't you just love it when things come together? Boy meets girl, eyes connect across the
room. Some things about life you can't make
up, they just happen serendipitously and that's
all there is to it. Beautiful.

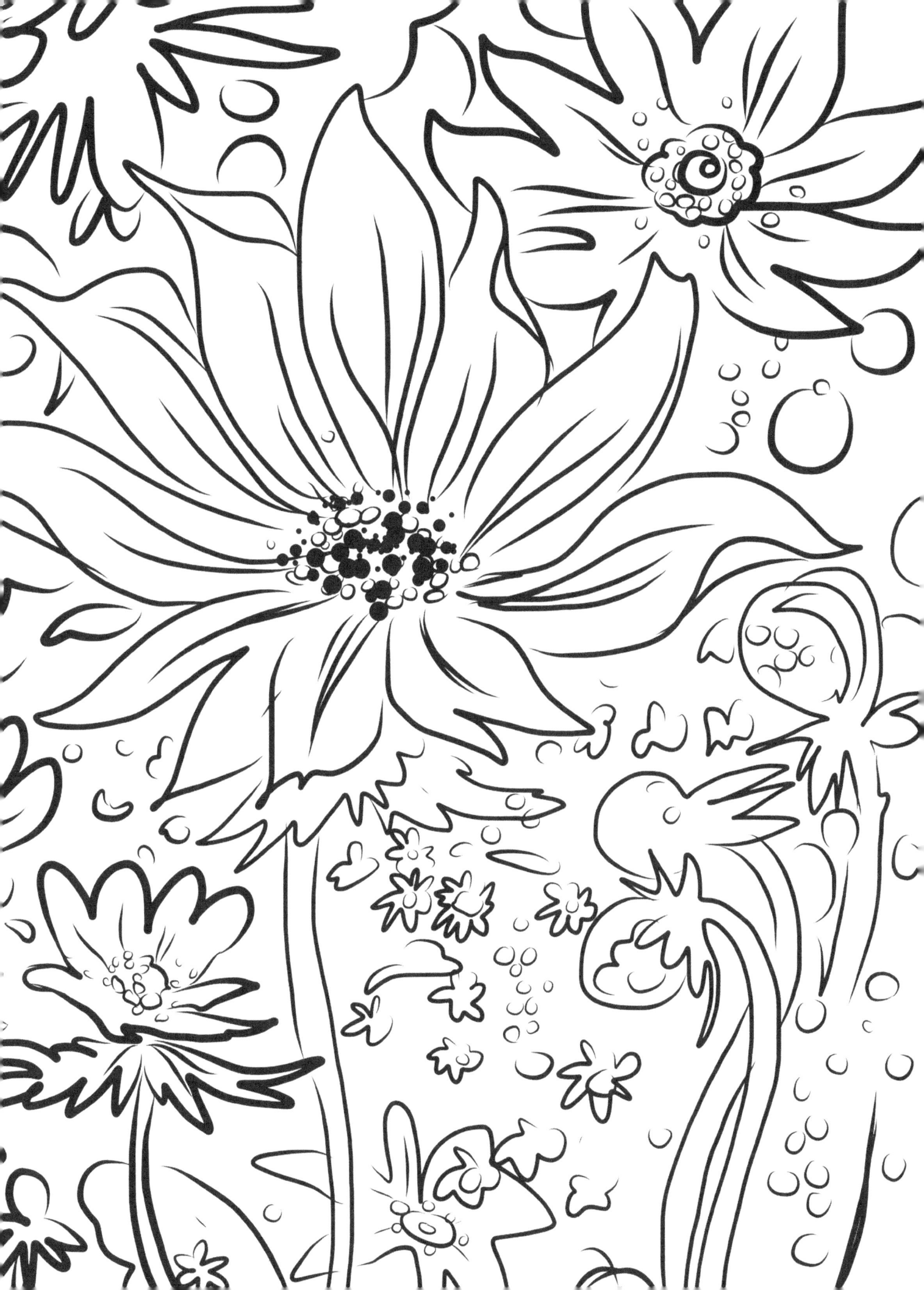

Angels

These four flowers remind me of guardian angels looking down on their charges with loving concern.

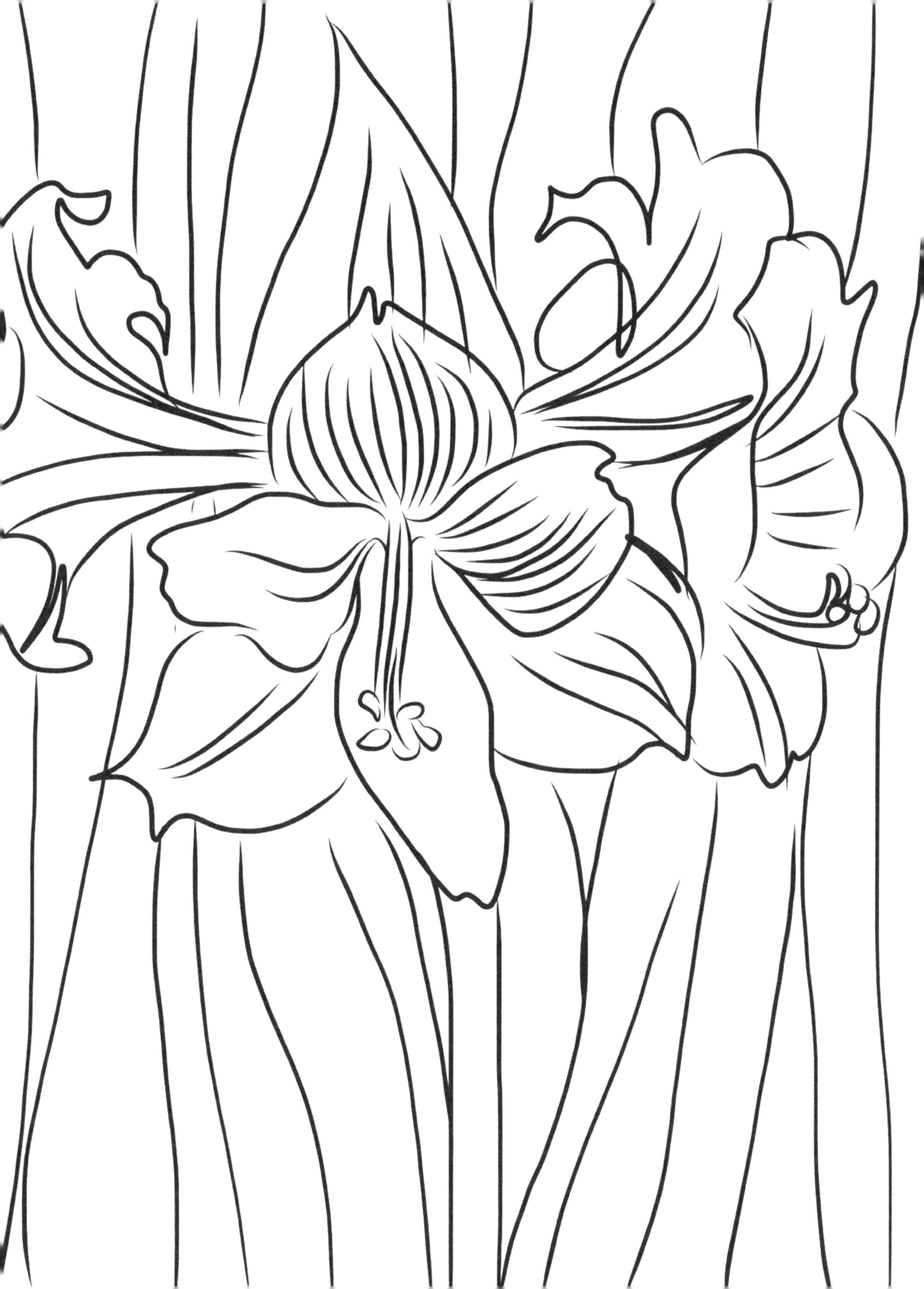

Flowers

The more I look into the deep mystery of flowers the more I seem to learn. The closer I look, the more I see. Their transient, intimate beauty enthralls me and takes my mind on a journey beyond the things that can be seen with the eye alone.

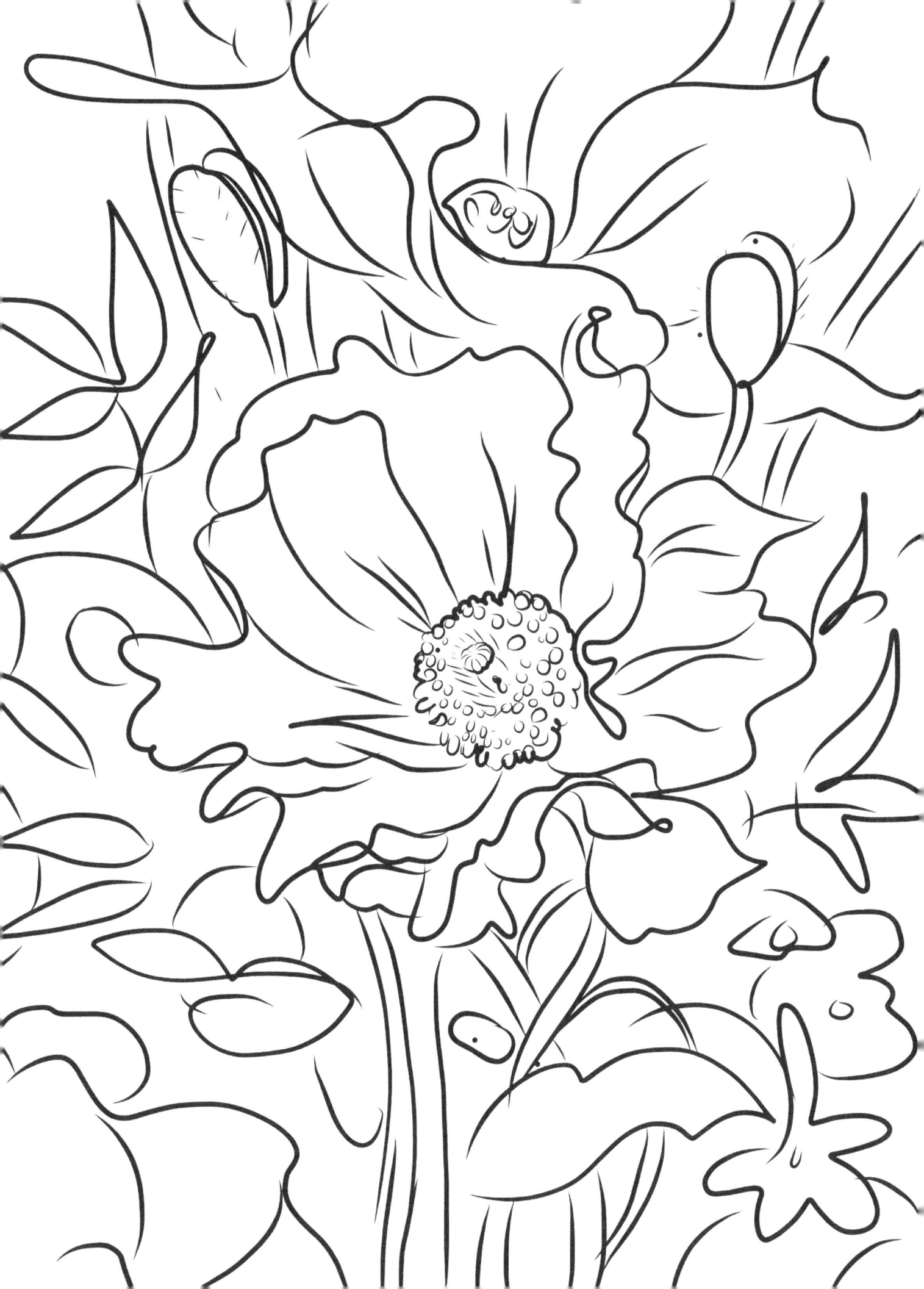

About the artist

Simon Bull's vibrant paintings are infused with a joy and humor that celebrates all that is good in life, whether it be a simple flower, a stunning heart, a glass of wine, or the flowing lines of a saxophone.

Artist and cancer survivor, Simon learnt the hard way the importance of celebrating life's great little moments as they happen. "I wanted my paintings to lift people's spirits, to send them on their way with a smile on their face, like a shot of caffeine in the morning."

His paintings have been featured on ABC Television's Extreme Makeover Home Edition, MTV Cribs, ShopNBC and on cruise ships worldwide. They have been introduced by Randy Jackson of American Idol, unveiled by Ashley Judd among others and can be found in many collections both public and private around the world.

Career Highlights

Official Artist - Salt Lake Winter Olympics.
Official Artist - Boxing Legend Muhammad Ali.
Multiple Award Winner - 'US Limited Edition Print of The Year'. NALED
Winner - 'Artist Print Award' Best selling printmaker in Great Britain.

Simon Bull resides in California.